# It takes
## a ~~village~~ *church*
## to raise a
### ~~child~~ *parent*

15 The Chambers, Vineyard
Abingdon OX14 3FE
**brf.org.uk**

Bible Reading Fellowship is a charity (233280)
and company limited by guarantee (301324),
registered in England and Wales

ISBN 978 0 85746 625 9
First published 2018
Reprinted 2019, 2021
10 9 8 7 6 5 4 3 2
All rights reserved

**Acknowledgements**
Scripture quotations are taken from The Holy Bible, New International Version
(Anglicised edition) copyright © 1979, 1984, 2011 by Biblica. Used by permission
of Hodder & Stoughton Publishers, an Hachette UK company. All rights reserved.
'NIV' is a registered trademark of Biblica. UK trademark number 1448790

Every effort has been made to trace and contact copyright owners for material
used in this resource. We apologise for any inadvertent omissions or errors, and
would ask those concerned to contact us so that full acknowledgement can be
made in the future.

A catalogue record for this book is available from the British Library

Printed and bound by CPI Group (UK) Ltd, Croydon CR0 4YY

# It takes a ~~village~~ *church*

# to raise a

# ~~child~~ *parent*

## Creating a culture where parenting for faith can flourish

## Rachel Turner

For Revd Tony Hurle, my wise women, and the entire church community of St Paul's, St Albans. This book began with you. Thank you for going on the ride with me.

# Contents

# Introduction:
# transforming our approach

The clink of mugs on tables and the faint laugh of friends muffled the air as parents, grandparents and a few children's and youth leaders gathered in the small chapel. It was the start of another Parenting for Faith course at my church. As the people settled, I started the session by asking them to share why they came.

A brave dad began the conversation. His voice wavered a bit as he spoke. 'I've been a Christian for over 20 years. To be honest, I feel that I barely share any of it with my children. I pray with my kids sometimes, but not daily. I'm ashamed to say I rarely pray for them when they're not around. We read a storybook Bible occasionally, but...'

He shifted in his seat. 'I have a 15-year-old, a 12-year-old and an 8-year-old, and I want my kids to have a faith, to know God. I just don't know how to do it. Or if it's too late.'

The room fell quiet for a moment, and then another man cautiously broke the silence. 'My son just started going to the local Church of England school and he comes home with all sorts of questions. I'm not even sure there is a God, but I want to help my kid figure this stuff out.'

An older mother piped up. 'I sort of feel like I'm coming from the opposite end. I have four children, and we do lots of Christian stuff at home. We pray before meals, read the Bible at bedtime, have family devotionals sometimes, when I remember. For some of my kids, I feel like they enjoy it and engage with God. For the others, I feel they think it's just activities to do. I want them all to own their faith, love God and want to be with him. Most of all, I want that feeling to grow and not fade when they get older.'

The woman next to her started to speak, but then she paused to choke back her tears. She began again: 'I feel like I'm ruining my kids' faith. I'm so tired. So, so tired. I'm so far from being the kind of Christian I want my children to see. I try, but I feel I'm screwing up more than helping!'

Around the room they went, one by one, sharing why they were there. Everyone was approaching the course from their own unique experiences and situations. Some had had childhoods where Christianity was forced on them or where their parents had no faith at all. Others were newly pregnant couples wanting to parent well. A few were drowning solo parents with multiple under-3-year-olds. Scattered throughout were godparents wanting to take their role seriously, parents with adult children in university navigating scary moments and grandparents who felt they failed in raising their children for faith and were looking at a second chance with their grandchildren.

Every time I run a course, I am amazed at the range of people who choose to attend. Our churches reach so many different parents and extended families, and our communities are so diverse. Yet despite these differences, the people all need the same thing: the encouragement and skills that will equip them to raise their children and teens to embrace a lifetime of relationship with God.

Olwyn Mark concluded in her compilation of 50 years of research studies that the most significant influencer of a child's faith is the child's parents, and yet only 36% of parents feel confident with that role.[1]

In other words, the ones who can make the most difference in the spiritual lives of children and teens are the ones feeling the most disempowered: the parents. This fact unfortunately coincides with the trend that we are seeing of children and young people leaving our churches at an alarming rate. If we are to see children and young people growing in faith and persevering with their relationships with God, then we as the church need to readjust our approach.

## The misalignment of discipleship

If we – the church – are to restore confidence to parents, then we first need to look at how we think about discipleship.

In recent years, the trend in Christian communities seems to have been towards believing that church services and programmes were the best places for children and teens to be discipled. Many factors over the past 50 years have contributed to this trend: Sunday school being held at the same time as church services, new waves in parenting methodology, and the professionalisation of youth and children's ministry, to name a few. The rate of growth of youth and children's ministry over the last 30 years has been ever upwards, with churches investing more and more time, people, resources and money into programmes to successfully instil faith into the next generation and to bring back youth who have walked away from God. As a result, churches have worked harder to provide better programmes to keep children and youth walking with God.

I started in ministry as part of this church-programme focus. I was a youth and children's pastor, passionate about children and teens loving God and knowing his love in return.

On some days, I admit, I arrogantly felt like superwoman. 'Behold! I am the Children's and Youth Pastor, holder of young people's spirituality in my hands! Send your children to me, and I shall turn them into Mighty Oaks of Righteousness. Look how your children love to come to church. Watch your youth return from Friday-night group singing worship songs. That's because of my awesome programme! Look at how your six-year-old can describe substitutionary atonement. That's my brilliant leadership in action. Just bring them to me, and I'll make it all okay. Tell me what you think your child needs, and I will make it happen!'

I wanted children and teens in the UK to know how valuable, loved, powerful and alive they were in relationship with God. I ran outreach groups, invested in schools work and ran a thriving Sunday-morning programme, just like many others in churches around the UK.

Then alongside this wonderful effort by churches across the nation, something unintentional and not so wonderful began to emerge. Parents began to believe that for their children to develop faith, their main job was to get their teens and children to these services and programmes. After a while, they began expressing frustration that the children's and teens' provisions at church were not frequent enough, good enough, or engaging and entertaining enough to ensure their children and young people wanted to keep going.

Dissatisfaction came from some church leaders and volunteers, too. They bemoaned how parents needed to get their children to their events more often, and how frustrated they were that parents didn't seem to access the resources and services that churches put on.

It seemed that despite the church's best efforts, the programmes were not producing the results they had hoped for. Clearly something wasn't working.

It appeared that a transformation of approach to discipleship was needed.

One weekend I went on a retreat to pray, and God brought me to Deuteronomy 6:4–9:

> Hear O Israel: the Lord our God, the Lord is one. Love the Lord your God with all your heart and with all your soul and with all

your strength. These commandments that I give you today are to be on your hearts. Impress them on your children. Talk about them when you sit at home and when you walk along the road, when you lie down and when you get up. Tie them as symbols on your hands and bind them on your foreheads. Write them on the door-frames of your houses and on your gates.

In an instant it hit me. I wasn't in any of those places in the lives of children and young people. I didn't lounge at home with them on their couches. I wasn't the one who walked down the road with them to school or drove them to swimming lessons. I didn't put them to bed or enjoy the casual boringness of a morning routine with them. I didn't hang out while they were getting dressed or when they decorated their homes.

I realised the church could not be the centre of children and young people's discipleship, because the home was perfectly positioned to be that centre.

I began some research, and I found that parents spend on average from 2,000 to 3,000 hours a year with their children, if they live with them. These hours include the ordinary parts of life: the journeys to and from events, the mornings together and the laughing together after dinner.

The church, on the other hand, has much less time with children per year. If children and young people show up every week to everything I run, I would see them for 100 hours a year. The time difference between what the church has and what parents have is massive.

If I wanted to see every child and teenager connected to God and discipled well, then I needed to get out of the way and focus on serving parents, because God designed discipleship to happen primarily throughout the day, every day, and especially in the mundane bits of life that only parents have access to.

As I began to develop this idea by talking with the parents in my church, I noticed something: we had all become content with a much smaller version of God's design for our children, families and church. In this smaller version of God's design, many children and teens were often growing up without the family discipling them. Many parents were missing out on some of the best parts of being a parent: helping their children know and love God, experiencing the peace and purpose of living authentically in front of them, and seeing that their own humble imperfectness would empower their children's faith. Moreover, many churches were missing out on the effectiveness and delight of having a powerful, purposeful community of all ages loving and serving God together. But we, as individuals and as a church, didn't have to settle for so little. We could help restore a fuller version of God's design, creating a culture where parenting for faith could flourish. We could bring back the joy of how God designed us, and place that joy back into the heart of our relationships and our churches.

Shortly after, I went on a journey of figuring out what Deuteronomy 6:4–9 meant for me and my ministry. I apologised to parents and began to reposition myself to serve them in their call as disciplers of their children and teens. I listened and learned what they wanted and what skills they needed, and I tried to find ways to equip them. I heard any and all of their insecurity and fears, and I figured out how to encourage them well.

On that journey, something developed that I never expected. Parents grew in their enjoyment of parenting and felt competent to help their children and teens navigate messy life with God. Both parents and children discovered new things of God and openly shared their discoveries with each other, encouraging one another.

Parents also began to support and disciple each other. People who had been parenting their children for faith began to pick up families who were new to it. Extended family and friends began to pick up and use the skills as well. Our church began to reflect these values and skills across our services and in our practice. Our community began to change.

I learned that when I was just focused on how I personally could grow a child's faith, my impact was limited. But when I began to encourage and equip parents, then they grew and, in turn, they had a greater impact on their own child's faith. Consequently, the whole community grew more connected to God.

## It takes a church

There is an old phrase: 'It takes a village to raise a child.' In several ways this saying is true. A village is committed to the flourishing of each child through the support it gives to those who are naturally a part of that child's world. The child is first surrounded by the parents, then embedded within an extended family, and ultimately embraced by the whole village community. The village doesn't *replace* parents or the extended family. The village *encircles* and *embraces* parents and the extended family in order to best support the children. The church needs to be that village if we are going to see parents flourish.

In modern society, with the fracturing of family, the increased frequency of people moving house, and the breakdown of close-knit community, the church is needed more than ever. It is needed to raise parents to embrace their role, and it is needed to restore the support surrounding a child and teenager so that parenting for faith can again flourish.

When a church does this well, something wonderful happens. I have seen it in churches up and down the UK and in communities all over the world. When a church embraces those surrounding and supporting a child and raises parents to flourish in parenting for faith, then good things begin to happen. We not only see children and teens run with God, but we also see adults filled with more encouragement and joy and extended families invested in each other more deliberately. We see church communities flourishing in their purpose, impacting their local community in outreach, and creating more opportunities for people of different ages to interact with each other. When a church changes, the lives of all those within its influence are impacted.

If we are going to see parents truly embracing their roles as the disciplers of their children, then we need to radically rethink our role as leaders in the church community.

We need to come to parents with a different heart – to see them freed to be all God has called them to be in the life of their child and to see their extended family and friends equipped to play their part – and with a commitment to be the church who will serve them, invite them and their children to belong and participate, and create for them the best environment in which they can be equipped to flourish. We need to do this so that we all might see a generation of children, teens and young people raised to know and love the Lord.

## What you will find in this book

If you are looking for '101 tips and activities for spiritually parenting', then I'm afraid you will be disappointed. Since 2004 I have worked with thousands of parents and hundreds of churches, and I have found that every situation is unique. No formula will always work. No programme can be guaranteed.

What I hope to do in this book is to give you the values and skills you need in order to pioneer in your context; to help you think about the parents you serve; and to give you the foundations you need to be ready to inspire, encourage, equip and walk alongside your parents. The principles in this book have been refined through a lot of experience, tons of mistakes, gracious partnerships, and much trial and error. All stories in this book are real stories of real parents, churches and leaders.

I hope this book will embolden you to find the right path for the parents you serve, so that as we all step into our roles to disciple each other, the church can and will flourish.

This book is divided into three parts – Vision, Skills and Church Culture – but it is really a book of two halves. The first two parts, which consist of the first six chapters, set out the approaches and skills we as individuals and leaders use in order to equip and support parents. The final part, the next six chapters, looks at the structural adjustments we need to make in church to create a culture where parenting for faith can flourish. I know many of us will want to skip to the final part, but I would encourage you not to. In my experience, doing the first six chapters without the final six can still be significantly impactful, but doing the final part without Parts 1 and 2 bears little fruit. The combination of both creates a fully functioning and significantly flourishing culture of parenting for faith.

I believe that one of the reasons God has placed us as church communities on this earth is to help people who love God become confident parents who can proactively, joyfully and lightly enable their children to grow in God-connection for a lifetime. It isn't something that just happens by itself. When people who come from so many varied backgrounds of faith are faced with having to transition into parents who parent for faith, then their deepest fears, worries and insecurities emerge. We have the privilege of being in places where we can help parents transform into who God has designed them to be in the lives of their children.

As a church we can do this, and we can do it well. It is never too late for parents and carers to start parenting for faith.

# Vision

# Introduction:
# creating a thirst and a hunger

Many successes in parenting are clear: getting children to walk, to feed themselves, to tie their shoes, to not lie, to obey the first time. Parents know what it looks like for their children to succeed at those things, so they know when they can pat themselves on the back for a job well done. They might not feel like they completely know how to get their children there, but they know the direction to go in.

When it comes to faith, though, many parents don't know what counts as success. Questions often fill their minds. Should I aim for my children to do faith things with me without complaining? Should they be reading their Bible on their own? If my children aren't praying out loud, does that mean their faith isn't strong? What about self-control: is that a reasonable 'fruit of the Spirit' for a four-year-old? Aargh!

Parents need help. We often jump to trying to get parents to do 'faith at home' when they don't know what that looks like in reality. Many of them are new to life with God, so they don't have childhood memories of a Christian home to draw from and build upon. Many parents have never met a five-year-old who genuinely loves God or a nine-year-old who is active in her faith, so they don't know what is possible. Before we equip parents to parent for faith, we have to give them a good idea of what is possible and what they can aim for.

Parents continually need to be enabled to have a vision for their family and for their children's spiritual lives. This vision is what motivates parents. It is what inspires them and gives them clarity for what is possible and available for their children. They need to be able to see what a child who loves God looks like and what a family who parents for faith can be like, and how normal it all can be.

When working with parents, you may notice there are two types: those who are already interested in parenting for faith and those who show little or no interest or urgency. Both need vision.

## Vision for those who are keen

Many of the parents we work with already have within them some desire to parent their children for faith. They may already be trying to do so in some way. They may pray with their children at bedtime or may have bought Bibles to read to them. They may bring their children to church and desire their teens to have a faith. They may very deeply want these things for their children, but often they don't know how to get their children completely 'there', or even know where 'there' is. This uncertainty results in many parents feeling either unmotivated, because they think they have reached the limit of what is possible for their children, or insecure, because they don't know how to enable their children to genuinely connect with God. These parents need a vision that inspires and ignites their desire to parent for faith so they can see their children's spiritual lives flourish.

I hate drinking water. I know I should love it, but I don't. Yes, I know it's good for me. Yes, I know my body is a billion parts water. Yes, I know about the wonderful joys of being continually hydrated. But you know what? I don't like water. I don't like the taste. I don't like having to wee a thousand times a day. If it were up to me, I would never say, 'Ooh, a big glass of water, please.'

Until I exercise. Then I can't get enough. Give it to me in the biggest bottle you have. I want to drink litres. I *need* it.

When I'm in the right environment, something shifts in me. The human need I already had for water intensifies drastically. More than just in my head – in my body, my senses, my heart, every part of me is screaming, 'Give me the water!' Exercise creates a need in me that I can feel. At that point, no one needs to lecture me on the benefits of water. I elbow people out of the way trying to get to the tap.

For parents who already know parenting for faith is important, we can create environments that make them thirsty to see their children connect with God and thirsty for themselves to flourish in parenting their children for faith. We can change their environment so they can see the possibilities for their children and for themselves. We can give them a vision they desperately need.

## Vision for the reluctant

You also have met the other type of parents. The parents who seem to be genuinely uninterested in helping their children develop a lifelong walk with God. Others may be holding themselves at arm's length because they think it's the church's job to be the spiritual provider for their children. They may even appear to be disengaged, too busy or too frazzled to care.

These parents need vision too, but in a different way. The first step is to give them a vision where they have none.

Marks & Spencer has this approach nailed. If you've ever seen the adverts on TV for M&S food, you will know what I'm talking about. In particular, I'm thinking of one of their puddings that was like a chocolate cake bomb. Cut into it and warm liquid chocolate oozed out. M&S wanted us to buy this chocolate cake. But they couldn't change our environment – they couldn't make us hungry or force us to purchase their food – so they decided to cast us a vision. Literally.

Picture the scene. It's your usual evening, watching *Britain's Got Talent*, and you're content, full after a lush tea and needing nothing. You have no desire for food in any way. All of a sudden, the screen goes black for a second. And then in HD the most gorgeous cake you have ever seen spins slowly before you. Classical music swells in the background as a silky-smooth deep voice rumbles, 'Dark. Moist. Rich.' A fork moves in slow motion towards the cake, and as it cuts through the delicate and springy sponge, decadently oozy chocolate flows out. 'Belgian chocolate with caramel dust transports you to the finest cafes in Europe.' You watch more slow-motion chocolate flowing as the announcer then delivers the coup de grace: 'It's not just food. It's M&S food.'

Before the advert, I had no desire for food. After the advert, I am poking my husband and exclaiming, 'I want that cake! We should get that! Look at it!' The first time I saw the advert, I actually went out of my way to pop into M&S the next day to ask an awkward clerk, 'Where can I buy that moist, dark oozy-cake thing from the telly?' The vision and description of the cake showed me something I didn't know existed. Once I knew what was on offer, I wanted it.

Many of the parents we work with appear to be apathetic about parenting their children for faith. In my experience, this perceived apathy is a result of parents not knowing what is possible for themselves and their children. They do not know how fulfilled and spiritually rejuvenated they will feel when they help their children connect with God in the midst of life, fear and worry. They may never have talked with a twelve-year-old who is facing bullying at school with the confidence that only comes from knowing the reality of God with him, so they don't even know that is available for their child.

Parents won't parent for faith effectively if they feel like they should. They will only do it effectively if they have a deep desire to be who they are called to be, if they feel inspired and capable to parent for faith, and if they know the pay-off in their children's lives is necessary, significant and attainable. I believe that God has placed within parents this desire to see their children connected to him. Even among non-believing parents, I see this desire. Our first job is to help uncover that desire, inspire it, and remove any barriers parents have to believing that parenting for faith is possible. By doing that, we can equip parents for the journey they want to go on.

The following chapters are about how we do this. How we can reposition ourselves to become a place of vision to enable parents, no matter where their starting point is, to become emboldened, focused and ready to parent their children for faith.

# 1

# Being Ikea

My earliest memory of going to a dentist seems burned into my brain. I'm sure I had been before this moment, but for some reason when I was nine years old it made an impression.

It was just a normal check-up, routine and boring, but I was heart-thumpingly nervous and a bit afraid. Not afraid of what the dentist would do to my teeth. Oh no, that was the least of my worries. I was afraid of being found out as a teeth-hygiene fraud. My hidden failures and secret cheats of only brushing my teeth for one minute instead of two and forgetting to brush the inside edge of my top ones would be discovered to have caused vast and lasting damage to my teeth. Forever. Hidden cavities would be exposed. I knew that on that day I would be found out.

When Dr Perfect flashed me his perfectly straight white teeth, I instantly knew that this was not going to go well. He and my mum chatted a bit, then he swivelled towards me with his glorious shiny mouth and asked the question I had been dreading. 'Do you brush your teeth two times a day?'

Relieved, I answered, 'Yeees.'

He nodded. 'For two minutes each time?'

I wanted to throw up. I thought, 'Do I lie? My *mum* is here. Can he tell the difference when he looks at my teeth?' I decided I'd go with a non-committal 'I think so.'

He flashed his blinding neon teeth again. 'Well, then, hop on up!'

And I knew in that moment there was no place to hide.

I still have this experience of the dentist. I go because I know it's important. I really do want teeth that last a lifetime. But the stress of exposure is still lurking in the background. The scenario nowadays goes something like this:

'Do you regularly floss?'

'Oh yes, absolutely.' I don't. That's a total lie. But I made a mistake once of telling the truth and the large lecture I got made telling the truth not worth it any more.

'Brush your teeth two times a day?'

'Yes, I sure do!' Unless I'm lazy or exhausted and accidentally fall asleep while putting my kid to bed, in which case I sometimes forget.

'Well, then, hop on up!'

Then I lie there, listening to my dentist assess my truthfulness. She calls out the numbers of my teeth, makes comments on where it's obvious I'm missing out in brushing. I feel embarrassed and agree to go through another tooth-brushing demonstration and listen to advice about when to drink juice.

I can't remember one time I emerged from a dentist appointment high-fiving the assistants and feeling like I nailed it. I usually emerge humbled and wiser, having faced my obvious failure and fairly sure I'm not going to improve much before the next encounter.

A dentist wants the best for us and our teeth. All their wisdom and experience is useful, necessary and exceedingly helpful for us in our lives. When we have a tooth crisis of pain, cavities or cracks, we are deeply grateful that dentists exist. And yet often, through no fault of their own, the very process of interacting with dentists can leave us feeling discouraged.

A dentist represents a big 'SHOULD' in our lives. We 'should' be taking care of our teeth in a detailed and prescribed way. So when we go to get our teeth checked and fixed, and we're sent back on to the straight and narrow of good dental hygiene, we feel slightly guilty and sensitive about it all.

I believe parents often feel this way about the church. The parents who want to see their children connecting to God feel like we are assessing their effectiveness and judging them as wanting. For them, church can become the place where their failures are exposed. The parents who aren't too bothered about parenting for faith brace themselves to endure the anticipated unwanted lecture of our view of which Christian things they 'should' be doing at home.

When parents need help with something their child is going through, like nightmares or the death of a family member, and they manage to ask a question, they brace themselves for the exposure. They often apologise in advance: 'I know I should pray more with them'; 'I wish we read the Bible more.' In asking for help, they can feel that we will inspect their failures and find them wanting. That's a big barrier to get past.

I know many people who only go to the dentist when the pain gets so extreme they can't stand it any more. For many of our parents, it is the same. They only seek us out when it begins to go wrong enough for them to overcome their aversion. Somehow, in our eagerness to help, parents can feel pushed, judged and never good enough. They can feel the 'should' of parenting for faith, and yet interaction with us leaves them feeling buried in a list of expectations and guilt.

If we want all the parents in our church to feel confident, capable and free from shame, then we need to shift our approach. We need to stop being the parenting-for-faith dentists. Instead, we need to be Ikea.

Ikea is a global retail chain with warehouse-sized stores that house a multitude of furniture, homewares, garden supplies and more. Everything you could ever think of needing for your home or office is in Ikea – at affordable prices. We walk along a winding path past little open rooms designed to look like a lounge or bedroom to show how vastly different homes could look with Ikea products. We walk and walk, almost on a journey of self-discovery.

'You know, I actually really like this,' we exclaim while stroking a feathered lampshade. 'Ugh, I hate that.' We roll our eyes at another kitchen counter. We see things we have never seen before and convince ourselves that we need them. Ikea flings open its doors and yells at us, 'You and your family are different from every other family in the world. Look at all the thousands of ways you can capture the uniqueness of your family in your home. Do you like this? Or this? What makes you happiest? What would work best for you?'

For many of us, we float through the experience filled with hope and joy of how we will go home and transform our kitchen with new storage jars and a new shelf that is so us. We look forward to Ikea trips. They are family events. We call our friends and tell them we are going and invite them along.

We church leaders need parents to see us like that, as people of encouragement and option, support and choice. We need parents to see us as a church where they are welcomed as a unique family, where they are shown many ways to parent for faith and where they can choose the options that work best for them. We need to stop being the dentists, ready to tell parents the exact formula of successful parenting for faith, and start being more like Ikea.

We need to start saying to parents, 'God has a great plan for your children and for you as a family. You are called and capable of parenting your child to know and love God. Parenting for faith will look different for every family because God designed it to be light and natural and reflective of you as a unique family. When you are ready, we are here to help you.'

When we do this, parents begin to relax. They feel less judged and less under scrutiny, and they become more proactive, more open and more intrigued because they have the choice. They can be set free to grow their vision for what is possible in their parenting lives and in the spiritual lives of their children, because we don't box them into our vision.

There is one key belief we need to embrace if we are to position ourselves well to encourage and equip parents: *there is no one right way of parenting for faith.*

Truly owning this belief will be hard for many of us. I include myself in that statement. I have written five books about how to help children and teens flourish with God in a complex world, so I have definite opinions about what works best and have my preferred methods. But when I work with parents, there is a core value I have that overrides those beliefs. It is the understanding that parents must choose a path for their family that they are convinced is right, doable and matches who they are. If they don't, then they will never truly implement their parenting-for-faith choices or embrace them with confidence.

We've all been pressured into buying something we don't want. We get it home and say, 'What in the world was I thinking? This thing isn't me at all!' When it comes to supporting parents, the instant killer is to have a hidden agenda. Parents can sniff an agenda a mile away. If we secretly believe there is one and only one way to parent for faith, then we will be very friendly but accidentally manipulative. We will try to twist parents' concerns or fears into ending up where we want them to be, and they will sense this and resist it.

Our job must be to help parents find the vision and skills that work best for them. Ikea truly doesn't care which of its products you choose. You don't get a sense that they like certain pieces of their product line more than others. You don't feel shoved towards one particular product over the others. Every time I go to Ikea, I see people leaving Ikea with something amazingly ugly that they love. Ikea's goal is that people will find something they love. They will buy and use it, and it will work for them.

My goal is for parents to find a vision and tools that they love, that they will learn and implement them, and in doing so that it will produce the fruit of spiritually alive children and passionate, confident parents. I'll bend over backward to help parents find that, even if I don't think it's the vision or the tools I would have chosen.

Operating out of this value is much harder than it sounds. Keeping our own opinions and preferences out of the centre as we help parents means we need to sacrifice. Sacrifice being the expert, having the power and wanting to manage the process of children's discipleship. Do I think my approach would be better? Yes. Do I think it would be more effective? Yes. But would parents implement my approach with as much joy, confidence and competency as the one they have chosen? No. And that's the heart of it: if my ideal solutions don't fit them well, then those solutions will be fruitless.

So, my challenge becomes how to give the parents I work with the options they need in a way that fits them as a family, so they can see their children connect with God.

It doesn't mean that the core truth changes, just the delivery method. It's like medicine. When you are ill, sometimes the remedy you need is a specific type of medicine. You need the one that will be most effective in giving you the results you want. When I had kidney stones (which, by the way, is absolutely as painful as childbirth; people are not lying), I was writhing in pain, vomiting and practically begging for help. One new doctor tried to sit me down and give me a little explanation of the medication she was giving me. 'We are going to order some morphine for you because you are in extreme pain. I prefer to give it in pill form.'

I managed to gasp out, 'But I'm being sick! I can't keep anything down and I really, really, really want the morphine right now!'

'Well, let's try it and see.'

At this point, I wanted to rip her face off. Tears were streaming down my face, and I was making grunting noises while shifting back and forth. 'Does it come in any other form?' I gasped.

'Oh yes, we can inject it through your cannula, give it through injection, or give it to you in liquid form to swallow. But I prefer the pill.' She smiled in an attempt to reassure me.

At this point, I transformed into the Hulk, and with the lowest gravelly voice I ever heard come out of me I said, 'I don't care what you prefer. Give it to me in the way you can guarantee my body will take it.'

One injection later, life was better. I needed pain relief, but I needed it in the way that would work for me. The medication was the same, but the method of delivery was different. There are many times in our ministries when we would prefer the parents we work with to do things in a specific way, but we need to remind ourselves of the key belief we need to operate out of: *there is no one right way of parenting for faith.*

When we fully embrace that, our hearts can be positioned to walk alongside each family and enable them to use the skills and values we give them to shape a way forward for their own unique style of parenting for faith.

# Lessons from Ikea

## 1 Create windows into normal life

One of the most powerful tools Ikea uses is the display room. They set up row after row of these rooms for people to explore. It is like walking onto a movie set. The rooms look so natural and lived-in, as if the owners had just stepped out for a moment. We can open their drawers and lounge on the couches. We can marvel at how they display their dishes on the shelves or how they cleverly store their shoes in the footstool. We get a glimpse into another person's life for a moment, and it makes us want to change bits of our own. We end up insisting to our friends, 'I would love to have that by my front door' and 'Isn't that a clever way to store stuff? I want one.' Without uttering a word, Ikea gives us a vision of what life could be, and then we naturally reflect on our own lives and ponder changes to our own homes.

In modern life, parents rarely get authentic insights into how other people parent, especially into how other families parent for faith. One of the most effective tools we have is our influence, which we can use to enable those places of observation and exchange to happen. When parents have opportunities to see into the lives of other people, they get a glimpse into various ways life could be and they ponder changes they might want to make in their own lives.

Chapter 3 focuses on the ways you can do this well. This is also part of the reason BRF created the website **parentingforfaith.org**. We wanted to have families of all shapes, sizes and church traditions create open windows into how they parent for faith, so other parents could look in and be intrigued at what it looks like for other people.

## 2 Display the range

Ikea is excellent at displaying its range of options. We arrive at the chair area, and displayed before us are hundreds of chairs in seemingly random order: bog-standard ones, cheap ones, beautiful ones, metal ones, wood-veneer ones, adorned ones and plain ones. They are all chairs, but which one you choose is down to your particular needs, restrictions and style.

When we try to give people a vision of what parenting for faith can look like in their family, we need to remember to present a wide range of options that they can implement. If we want to suggest, say, that parents discuss their children's media with them, it is easy to come up with one suggestion. Whatever that suggestion is, half the parents will think, 'That makes me cringe; it won't work with my kid.'

Instead, we can give parents a core value and show them the range of things they can do with it. Ikea says, 'Chairs are relaxing and necessary. Choose which one you like best.' We can say to parents: 'Engage with your children about what they are watching. It's really useful in shaping how they spiritually process the messages the world gives them.'

We can then give parents a range of options to choose from. We can say, for example:

> Children and teens are surrounded by media all the time. When we teach them how to process those messages with God, we can give them the skills they need to protect their minds, engage with lies and find the best in the media that is out there. But how you engage your children simply comes down to what you enjoy and what works best for you.

> If your children shut down when you're talking about what they're watching, then you may want to start by mentioning in the car about your favourite show when you were a kid and how it impacted how you played and what you dreamed about. If your family likes a good debate, then why not pick a movie you've been on the fence about watching and debate about whether it is good for your hearts and why, and what are the

pros and cons of how that movie may affect each member of your family.

If you need a more casual approach, you may want to try a drop-in the next time you walk through a room while your child is watching a show. As you walk past, casually mention one thing you like about the characters in the scene you just saw. 'I loved how they had each other's backs! You know I often pray that you will have friends who protect you like they protected each other in that show.' And then walk away. If your family are more cuddle-and-talk people, then as you put your child to bed at night, wonder out loud, 'You know how in that show we were watching today, Serena went back and apologised for pretending she didn't know Sarah? It reminded me of that story in the Bible when Peter did that to Jesus. Has that ever happened to you?'

When we give parents a range of options, they begin to see that there isn't one right way. There is just *their* way. I find that sometimes parents don't pick up any of my suggestions, but they invent their own way forward. Sometimes just seeing the options they don't like helps them to decide what they do like. I'm fine with parents rejecting all my ideas if it gets them thinking and finding their best way forward. In Chapter 6, we will be talking more about these skills.

## 3 Let people try things out

At Ikea, customers are able to try out everything – in a ridiculous way. I love going because I lie on the beds, sit in the chairs, try out the desks, and pretend to type on invisible computers at the kitchen counter. I open all the cupboard doors and try the awesome sliding shelves. Before I can decide whether something will work for my family, I must try it out without having to commit to it first.

In the same way, if we want to be like Ikea, we need to create a culture where people can try things; that is, a culture where they don't expect everything to work for them, but where they can be engaged in the process of discovery, trials and testing to see what best fits.

You may need to communicate to parents:

> Every family is different, so don't get discouraged if something you try doesn't work. Parenting is about trying things and finding what works best for you and your kids. Remember when you tried to get your child to sleep when he was a baby? You read books about techniques and even tried a few of them: you let him cry, carried him around all the time, stroked him, left him alone and played soft music. You tried many techniques and discarded the ones that didn't work. But you didn't give up hoping for and working towards good sleep. And eventually you found something that worked.

> It's the same with this. I'm here to keep giving you options and helping you find what works for you and your family, if you need it. But don't worry if it all doesn't work perfectly the first time. I'll still be here to help you find more options and help you refine what you have. You are the parent of your child. You will find the right tool to help your child connect with God in this situation. You are doing great.

Besides working one-on-one with parents, the church can also create spaces for people to try something new together. Invite parents into your kids' groups and let them try a new technique. In all-age services, add moments in which parents can experiment with new skills and tools. Give resources and challenges during a Parenting for Faith course, so people have a place to come back to and laugh and talk about the latest new thing they tried. In Part 2 we will be talking more about these specific skills.

## Vision is the gateway to function

If you have ever purchased furniture from Ikea, chances are that it was flat-packed and you had to assemble it yourself at home. But when you come into Ikea, you aren't met with a catalogue of one picture and 40 pages of assembly instructions. No one at Ikea is saying, 'Hello? Looking for a difficult, marriage-testing construction experience? You should try the Ypperlig. It's tough!'

The focus at Ikea isn't on the skills you need for the hard work of assembling the item. It's on the vision and functionality of the final item. In the store you are met with a vast floor of fully constructed models to look at and nosy around and be excited about. Only when you have fixed your vision on an item and made your own choice, then, and only then, are you willing to bring it home and construct it. Only then are you willing to take hold of the instructions and the skills and the supplies you will need. Only then, as you picture the final product, are you willing to put in the hours of hard work to see your vision become reality in your home.

Too often we rush our parents into the skill phase, and in doing so we can miss out on the crucial step of helping them cultivate their vision for their family and their children's connection with God. Like Ikea, we need to give parents plenty of opportunities to dream, to imagine and to experience parenting for faith differently. Only after they have a vision will they be willing to embrace the skills and the work needed to see their vision become reality.

When parents encounter us as a church wholeheartedly encouraging them to be envisioned for what God could do in the lives of their children and in their own parenting-for-faith journey, then they can step into the future with hope.

# 2

# Speaking truths

We live in a world of experts. Parenting often becomes about coordinating the right batch of experts to give our children the best possible chance for success. This juggling act begins early. First-time parents read as many books as they can from a wide variety of experts, looking for help in getting through those first few months with their newborns. As children grow, parents continue to seek out experts. Most send their children to schools so they can benefit from educational specialists. They take their children to doctors, bring in sports coaches and music teachers, work with additional-needs coordinators, and more. We shouldn't be surprised, therefore, when parents also view the church as another place to seek out experts, spiritual experts, who can help their children succeed along their journeys of faith.

In the last chapter, we looked at how Ikea encourages us to believe we are all experts in knowing what fits best in our own homes. Without that confidence, we would not be able to hold on to a vision or to stick with a decision about a product to take home and construct. In the same way, we need to encourage parents to see that they are the experts in their own families and homes. They are the knowledgeable ones who are best positioned to help their children succeed along their journeys of faith.

It's a big leap for parents to understand that, though they may be less skilled, less sure, less theologically trained, they actually are more effective and more impactful than 'experts' in the church. It takes a lot of courage for parents to believe that they are the foundation of God's plan for the spiritual lives of their children and teenagers (Deuteronomy 6:4–9). It takes a lot of confidence for parents to believe that, in their imperfectness and busyness, they are still crucial in God's plan for their children's spiritual journey.

It turns the culture of expertise on its head.

We need to take our parents on a journey of restoring truth in their lives. We need to reinforce through our words and actions that parents already have the expertise most needed for discipleship – they *know* their children and teens. They know what makes them tick and what makes them fearful. They know their moods, their worries, their secret strengths, their inner potential and their shining character traits.

Parents' connection, position and willingness to parent for faith is worth much more than spiritual expertise. We need to shape ourselves into truth-tellers, emboldening parents to see themselves as vital, capable and important in the spiritual lives of their children.

## The 'should' kryptonite

Many of you reading this book may be frustrated. You may be saying, 'I've been telling parents for years that they are the primary disciplers of their children. Parents get it. They know their role. They just aren't doing it!'

I understand the frustration. I have been there.

One big mistake we can make in trying to encourage parents is to give them only one message: 'It's not us; it's you. It's not the church's job to disciple the kids; it's yours. Off you go!' We say it in lots of ways: 'We believe parents are the primary disciplers of their children' or 'It's the parents' job to pass on their faith to their kids.' It's a one-message campaign: 'Do faith at home!'

In my experience, this single message triggers a massive guilt response from parents.

Parents feel guilty a lot – about a huge variety of things. A myriad of 'shoulds' live in their heads, and they often feel they are failing to do what is expected of a 'good' parent: 'I should be playing with my child three hours a day, and I'm not. I'm a rubbish parent'; 'I should be cooking with organic food all the time'; 'I should be able to afford better clothes for my kid'; 'I should take them out more.' These 'shoulds' weigh parents down and make them feel as if they are failing. Social media makes the matter worse by giving them access to images of 'perfect' parents doing vastly creative activities, parenting in ways they wish they could, and the comparison can be crushing.

So when we push parents to 'do faith at home', their guilt reflexes come in strong: 'I should be reading my Bible with my kids'; 'I should be better at praying with them'; 'I should do mission with them'; 'I should be teaching them about Jesus.' They can begin to feel isolated and afraid, and they believe the consequences for their failures will be the sacrifice of their children's and teens' walk with God.

Remember Superman? He would be going through his usual heroics until he was exposed to kryptonite. When Superman was near it, he would be overwhelmed with pain, sapped of strength and unable to continue. Feelings of 'should' are like kryptonite to parents. They will never effectively parent for faith if they are being burdened by the guilt and fear these expectations cause.

## The key truths

Parents need us to be truth-tellers. They need us to wade in and give them the confidence and solid ground to truly embrace who they are and the life that God has called them to.

Rather than communicate that parents are the primary disciplers of children and teens, and that they should do faith at home, try these key truths:

- God has given you a place of significant influence in the spiritual lives of your children, and that place cannot be replicated or replaced. Here are the reasons why: 1) influence happens through personal connection, and you have a longer and stronger personal connection with your children (including your teenagers) than anyone else has; 2) God is real in the everyday, so faith is applied every day; our relationships with God are woven into those everyday boring bits of life, and only you are present in those moments.
- No matter how hard the church tries, we will not be as effective as you can be. Even working super hard, we'll always be less efficient than you, doing parenting for faith casually and imperfectly.
- God knows what parenting is like. He knows parenting is busy, exhausting and tiring. He knows that on a good day, most of us are operating with half our energy and with exhausted brain power. He designed parenting for faith to be a light, natural, joyful and gritty part of everyday life. He designed you to be able to do it even when you are not functioning at your best.
- What children need most is to see what a real relationship with God looks like up close and in the everyday. They need to see it when bad things happen and when boring life rolls on and on. They need to see it when you witness something beautiful and when you hope for something big. Children need to be invited into the reality of the everyday, and only you can give them that invitation.
- How you parent for faith will be different from how others do it, because you are you and because you are the experts on your children. We want you to find your own style and path of parenting for faith that feels the most natural and productive to you. We will walk with you and give you the skills, values and approaches you need to shape your style. Comparison steals joy. Don't compare your unique path to others. Delight in yours.

- You are already doing loads of useful and significant spiritual discipling. We are just here to help you add to the good you are already doing.
- Relationship with God is a journey. None of us would say, 'Yes! I have reached the pinnacle of my relationship with God. It will never get any better than this. I have achieved perfection in how I do my life with him.' As long as you are on a journey in your relationship with God, you can parent for faith well. You don't have to go fast; you just have to be moving forward.
- Your children are on a journey too. Your job is to help them walk well by listening to them, by letting them see a bit of your experience and by sharing tips and skills that have helped you negotiate your walk with God.
- There are no guarantees. Your children are their own people. Your job is not to produce perfect Christian children who turn into perfect Christian adults. Your job is to parent them to the best of your ability, giving them everything they need to find their own personal connections with God and equipping them to walk their journeys of life with him.
- You are not alone. Our job is to cheer you on, have your back, support you, and help you to have all the skills you feel you need to do this well. We are *here* for you. We are *for* you. We are *with* you. How can we help?

When we communicate these truths, we place courage in the hearts of parents. We bring hope and restore possibility. If we can learn to lay these foundations for our parents, we can help them create a vision for now and for the future that inspires and motivates them to take the next steps.

**3**

# Enabling a community of stories

We are moved by personal stories. They often inspire us and help us to *aspire* to change for the better.

In everyday life, parents are surrounded by families and their stories. Parents love getting together with extended family and friends and talking about their children and teens. Through these natural conversations, there is also significant learning going on.

Take the topic of getting babies to sleep. When parents prepare for this challenge, they often draw on the stories of others. They recall watching their friends trying to 'sleep train' their children, or they look for YouTube videos of people sharing their experiences. Of course, parents will talk to everyone who has ever tried to survive the night with children and ask them about the approaches they tried and what happened. While gathering these stories, parents embark on their own sleep adventures with their own unique child. They start with their best guess for what will work, and after a while they re-evaluate and modify or replace techniques that don't work well. Along their own journey to blissful nights, parents gain stories of their own.

Whether it's about getting babies to sleep, securing the right appointment for a child with additional needs or choosing a secondary school, parents seek out each other's stories to gain wisdom and advice.

But when it comes to faith, there seems to be silence. After church, the question, 'So how is your child doing spiritually?' is seldom asked, if at all. Parents rarely talk about how they helped their child process with God about the death of a pet or how catastrophically wrong the first baptism conversation went. They can be hesitant to share how they are praying with their kid or how they are dealing with their teen's recent decision that God isn't real. Nevertheless, these stories are vital for parents to share with each other, for several reasons:

- they normalise parenting for faith;
- they inspire people in what real faith in children looks like;
- they remove the fear of failure;
- they encourage parents that children can truly love God and know his love;
- they share wisdom of how to help children through profoundly rough times.

## The red herring of activity

In the past, many of us have tried to harness parents' stories and share them. We spot parents trying new resources at home, praying together for people or going on a mission, and we share those tips and activities with others. Frustratingly, some of us have found this adds to our parents' guilt, rather than emboldening them. We know stories are crucial to helping parents develop a vision, but we can't quite figure out how to surround them with the right stories to ignite that vision.

I believe this is because we need to shift *which* stories we are facilitating and *how* they are shared.

In our effort to encourage parents, we often jump straight into wanting them to *do* something. So, we highlight the stories of parents doing things: reading Bibles, doing devotionals or having gathered times at home. We share stories of their actions.

But if parents truly were focused on just *doing* things, then their conversations would sound quite different. Parents would be shrugging their shoulders and saying, 'Well, I sat my son down and taught him how to tie his shoelaces. He seemed not to get it. Oh, well. I did my bit.' Or, 'I tried to toilet train my kid. Didn't take. Guess she's in nappies for a lifetime.'

In fact, parents are less focused on *doing* the right thing and more focused on trying to parent in a way that *will produce* the desired feelings and behaviour in their children. They match their deeply held values of *how* they want to parent with what they know *works* for their children, and then they find their own path to achieving their goals.

Parents share more stories about what they are trying and how it is working, than lists of what activities they are doing. Since that's the case, we need to shift our focus to facilitating stories of process.

Parents learn from hearing each other's choices, watching how each other adjusts and seeing how each other's children grow and change. For example, parents hear that their friends let their toddler sleep in bed with them, in order to get a night of uninterrupted sleep. They may think that they could never do that, until they also hear that their friends are sleeping eight hours a night and now have a non-grumpy child. Then, that technique might not sound so crazy. The parents may not try it if it clashes with their other values, but it opens them up to seeing more options and it helps them clarify their own choices.

## A community of healthy stories

In the same way, we as leaders can facilitate a community in which stories that truly equip and inspire people in their parenting for faith are shared.

Parents need access to a diverse community to laugh with, learn from and agree with, so they can reflect on how they would do things differently. This community is vital to parents developing a vision for their family and for the spiritual lives of their children. One of our roles is to help build a community that enables a flow of stories parents need to hear. Not stories of 'top tips', but stories like these:

1   **Stories of children and teens connecting with God** – Parents want their children to develop lifelong connections with God, so we need to feed them stories that focus on what God is doing in the lives of children and teens. These stories tell them what is possible, what God's heart is for life with him, and what is on offer to their children. These stories function like the M&S advert; they say, 'This is what your child can have.'

2   **Stories to convey 'trying'** – Parents often only hear stories that have already reached their conclusion, which can make them feel they're the only ones who still don't have it sorted. When we facilitate stories of the struggles parents are experiencing right now, we create a community of people who are on the journey together. When parents share what they are trying and what spiritual fruit they are seeing or not seeing, others in the community become invested in those journeys. We create a community who are for each other, who are asking about each other's progress, and who are sharing the joys and heartbreaks together. If we want to normalise parenting for faith, we need to enable a community to talk about it as if it were as ordinary as the rest of parenting: funny, tiring, disappointing, joy-filled and, most of all, unique to each individual.

3   **Stories of the up-and-down journey** – Parenting is an ever-changing process. One day something works, and for the next two weeks it's brilliant. Then the season changes, and what used to work no longer does. That is normal. Up-and-down stories can give hope to parents when they're facing changing times in their own families. Through these stories, parents can appreciate the beautiful spiritual fruit that is produced in their children during those seasons of growth. They can see the fruit as steps

in their children's journeys with God, and they are reminded to keep asking themselves, 'What is the next step for my children spiritually, and how can I help them take it?'

4  **Stories to laugh about and encourage** – Parenting comes with stories of hilarious failures. The internet is full of funny memes, videos of outrageous situations and parenting gone awry. Failure is a normal part of the parenting journey. But when it comes to their children's faith, parents often have little grace for themselves. When we enable families to tell stories of when things didn't go according to plan, we can help take away the fear and shame so many parents feel when they mess up. If we can enable parents to tell stories of their wild moments of spectacular failures, then they can lighten each other's hearts with moments of laughter.

5  **Stories to reflect all different sorts of socioeconomic and family structures** – Parents come to us with very different experiences and backgrounds. It's important that they not only hear stories that are similar to their own, but also are challenged by hearing stories that are vastly different. Too often our single parents can feel isolated when they only hear stories of happy two-parent families. Our poorer members can feel judged when they only hear stories of families who can freely buy resources or have great experiences on holidays. We can accidentally point to families in which both parents are Christians, instead of families with only one parent who is, or we neglect to tell any stories of children with additional needs. For parents to feel hope, they need to see their experience and circumstances reflected in stories around them. It is our job to bring those stories and to build communities that enable everyone to feel accepted, normal and partnered with.

## How to facilitate a community to share stories

There are a few skills we can use to facilitate parents to share their stories well so they can fuel each other's vision to invest in helping their children connect with God.

## Specific rather than vague questions

When we put parents together, we often try to create openness by asking broad questions to initiate conversation: 'What does doing "faith at home" look like for you?'; 'How do you help your children read the Bible?'; 'What have you found most successful in helping your child connect with God?'; 'What are your top tips for helping teens with media?' We want parents to feel that they are doing well, but in doing so we open the conversation with questions about success, which is not helpful.

If our goal is to have parents share stories that truly create companionship, mutual learning and a vision, then one of the best skills is knowing how to ask questions that release the right stories. Here are a few examples:

- 'Sometimes we all need encouragement, and we need to hear some stories of what God is doing in the lives of our children and teenagers. Would anyone be willing to share a story of a child you know who connected with God recently? I'll go first. A few days ago I was hanging out with my nine-year-old nephew, and it started to rain. We ran under a tree to shelter, and we just stood there for a while. Then out of nowhere he said, "I love the rain. Makes me feel small and surrounded by God's bigness." It was so cool to get that glimpse into his life with God for a moment. Anyone else?'
- 'We've been talking about helping our children and teens take their next steps on their journey with God. What is your kid's season right now, and what have you been trying? What is the fruit you are seeing, or not seeing?'
- 'Did anyone have a terrible parenting-for-faith week? I'm sure you aren't alone. We'd love to hear about it. Anyone have a breakthrough with something? Anyone get a glimpse into your child's journey that surprised or encouraged you? Any epic failure stories?'
- 'Susie mentioned she is new to this whole thing and feels like helping her child connect to scripture. She believes it's her kid's

next steps. Has anyone here been on that journey with a child and is willing to share? What is your child's personality like, and how did you arrive at that season? What did you try? What was God doing then, and how did your child's connection with God build during that time?'

When we ask specific questions, we can ensure that we are facilitating the stories that will inspire and encourage. Eventually, we will create a culture where people know which stories to share and how, but until people are naturally conversing this way, our questions provide a vital help.

## Progress stories are fantastic

Christians often feel that faith stories need to be big: for example, being saved out of homelessness or healed out of a wheelchair. We can often self-censor the smaller stories of personal growth and moments of connection that are so significant to us because we feel they are unimportant to others. Christian parents tend to do this when it comes to talking about faith as well. They don't share the little story of how their child who had always refused to pray at bedtime finally managed to sit through a time of prayer for the first time in three weeks. They don't want to share because that small success feels so insignificant in the grand scale of Christian testimony. But in truth, the triumph was a huge moment for that child and for that parent.

Having a community around parents who will see, affirm, pray for and rejoice with them is essential as parents walk through tricky seasons with their children. It is not only encouraging for the parents, but it also inspires those who get to hear what everyday life is like for others with children.

As we make it easier for parents to share their stories in community, we are able to ensure these progress stories will be prominent.

## The value of creating windows

One of the skills we teach parents is the concept of 'creating windows' into their lives with God so their children can see what a normal life with God looks like. When parents know how to create windows into key places in their lives, children and teens can see where God is active and how their parents respond to him in the everyday. It's a skill that is foundational for parents to understand and become comfortable with.

When parents truly understand that their own imperfect walks with God are powerful examples in the lives of their children, they can also understand that their own imperfect stories can be significant in the lives of other parents. As we encourage parents to authentically share all types of stories from their parenting for faith journeys, we can reinforce that all their journeys are worthy of being shared so others can learn. If you are at the beginning of creating a culture of openness, our website, **parentingforfaith.org**, can help. It has a steadily growing pool of videos and blogs of families sharing their stories on a myriad of topics.

## Facilitating stories well

An excellent place for vision to grow is in a community of parents, extended family and friends who are all journeying alongside each other and sharing their stories of the joys, pains, successes and failures. This community becomes a safe place for parents to dream about what is possible for their children and family and to begin to see a way forward for themselves – not alone, but together. The better we can facilitate stories in community, the more opportunities parents have for their vision to grow.

# Skills

# Introduction:
# the four essentials

I have often encountered the belief among Christian leaders that if parents just loved God enough, then they would naturally know how to raise their children to love God. Unfortunately, I do not think that is true. Many of the biblical 'heroes of faith' raised children who were disconnected from God: one of David's sons raped his sister and another son led a rebellion; Eli's sons were corrupt; Samuel's children were so bad the Israelites demanded a king; Jacob's children sold their brother into slavery; and on and on. Faith doesn't just trickle down by proximity and osmosis. This is because faith isn't just a belief system, it's a relationship with a living being. Relationships cannot be replicated or simply passed on.

The language of 'passing on' our faith to our children can focus parents on the wrong outcomes. If parents focus on 'passing on' their faith, then the quality, perfection and failings of their own journeys come into sharp focus. Success can then become about their children accurately replicating the good bits of what the parents themselves have. We are looking, however, for our children and teens to develop their own authentic, independent connection with a living God, out of which their behaviour and character will flow. Parents are still on their life's path of faith, and their children's journeys will be as unique as their parents' have been. The skills that the church gives to parents are not to help them 'pass on' their faith, but to enable them to confidently help their children develop their own.

Once parents have the *vision* to help their children have a connection with God, they need a set of core skills to empower their children. In an ideal world, they will have learned these skills from their own parents and the wider Christian village around them, but in many cases these skills have been lost or warped along the way.

When parents feel they don't have the spiritual skills they need, they reach out for a ready-made product to fill the gap. They begin to trust in pre-packaged tools that will act as substitutes for the natural skills they might have used. We have overwhelmed parents with tools to use with their children: books, Bibles, games, devotionals, apps and more. Many of these resources are excellent, and in general there is nothing wrong with them – I've written many myself. But many parents have become reliant on these tools to do the spiritual parenting for them.

Our goal is to train parents in the core skills they need so they know how to help their children or teens take the next step with God, with or without a resource in hand. When we do this well, books, CDs, DVDs and apps become a choice for them to use, ignore or adapt, rather than the only tools they think will work.

Training people can take a while. It isn't like handing out candy; it's like teaching someone how to drive. Teaching someone how to drive involves not just giving them the rules of the road, but steadfastly training them in the skills and habits needed to operate the vehicle, and helping them to be comfortable with unpredictable situations, so that no matter what happens, they can respond well.

Our job is to train parents in skills that they can apply to any and all situations, so they can face the challenges of parenting for faith head on. We need to train parents in these four essential areas:

- How to build connections with their children
- How to position themselves to influence their children's faith
- How to proactively disciple their children
- How to develop their children's connection with God in prayer

## Build connections

In 2017 Care for the Family published a study highlighting that the more connected a child feels to his or her parent, the greater the chance of a child's faith to take root and last.[2]

Some of the most important skills we need to give parents are in making and maintaining emotional connections with their children. On the face of it, this seems minor and easy. Kids love their parents, even in complex family situations, and parents can come to rely on this underlying love. But love doesn't necessarily mean connection.

Connection comes with trust, a sense of safety, emotional openness and affirmation, and a sense of profound care. Connection is something that takes deliberate cultivation. It is the core out of which influence arises.

One of our jobs as the church is to help equip our parents to build a connection with their children. The parents we serve come from a variety of homes and parenting backgrounds. Some of them don't know how to build a genuine connection with their children or how to maintain it through stress, the teen years, or while disciplining.

Parenting for faith isn't an add-on to normal parenting; it is intertwined with it. If we want people to easily and smoothly parent for faith, we will occasionally need to wade into talking about general parenting skills, which is where this area of building healthy connections regularly pops up.

## Position

Recently, a friend and I were trying to fix the legs back on to a big armchair. I sat down next to the chair to hold it in place as my friend screwed supports in, but it wasn't quite working. I was in the right location, but every time he pushed against the chair, it still moved a bit, no matter how much I tried to steady it, so the screw didn't go in right. It was frustrating. I asked him to pause, and I repositioned my body. I shifted a bit to the side, wrapped my legs around the base and braced my arm against the wall. Then we tried again. This time our effort was smooth and efficient. In the beginning I had placed myself in the right location and mostly positioned myself well. But after I reassessed our progress and made a few slight changes to my position, we managed to accomplish our task easily.

Parents are already in the right location in their children's lives, and most are already well positioned to influence their children for a life of faith. But with slight changes to their positioning, they will have much more impact.

Parents often feel paralysed when deciding where and how to position themselves to spiritually influence their children. Are they the spiritual leader, anti-sin enforcer, hands-off observer, question-answerer or something else? It is crucial for us to wade through their confusion and help them understand who they are in God's design for their families and how they can powerfully position themselves to influence the spiritual development of their children.

## Disciple

It is common sense that it takes specific skills in order to teach or disciple effectively. Teachers go through years of education to learn how to teach well in order for their students to have the best opportunities to excel. Coaches learn specific techniques and earn qualifications so they can enable their athletes to reach high levels of achievement. Ordained ministers have to go through years of theological research and approval processes from official organisations in order to work in their pastoral roles.

So often parents arrive at a moment to disciple their children, and then sense that they do not have the training or the skills to follow through with it. When we can equip parents with the specific skills to effectively disciple their children, we enable them to be the people God calls them to be. They grow in their confidence of being able to apply the general skills of parenting for faith to their specific family.

But for parents to be most effective, we need to equip them in ways that will help them the most. When driving instructors train learner drivers, they focus on the core skills drivers need to negotiate any road or circumstance they may face in the future. They don't take them down every road, micromanaging their learning on each one. In the same way, we need to focus on giving parents the general skills of how to approach problems, rather than the nitty-gritty specifics of what to do in each individual situation. We need to train them in the general core skills of how to perceive, think and respond, so they can adapt those skills to any circumstance they may face in the future.

## Developing God-connection in prayer

At the heart of each child's connection with God is a prayer life – where a child and God connect heart-to-heart. If our children don't have that, then they are missing the heart of faith.

Parents often see prayer as a huge mountain they struggle to climb as they enable their children to connect with God. It is the most obvious expression of a person's relationship with God, and yet it is among the least controllable from a parent's point of view. At its core, prayer is about individual, independent conversation with God. Parents need the skills of how to help children authentically share with God in whatever ways work best for those children. Parents also need skills in how to be aware of God's communications in everyday life, and how and when to separate corporate prayer from that personal, individual connection.

This often brings up parents' own vulnerabilities with prayer, as we are all on our own journeys and, therefore, in different places in our experiences with prayer. When we are willing to enable parents to discuss these issues, voice their personal journey, develop the skills to flourish in prayer, and release their children into a free and easy life of communication with God, then we can bless a whole family.

## What exactly are the skills parents need to know?

What is the specific list of core skills for each of these four essential areas? The answer is that there are no definitive lists. We will always continue to grow and expand ways to help parents develop their core skills in these areas. Over the years I have developed, and am still developing, a set of skills that I feel helps parents, some of which I mention in this book. But you also will bring to the table your own wisdom as you teach parents in these four areas. Some skills you might have picked up from wise parents you work with, or other skills you have already developed and use in your ministry. You may have skills you were given by your parents that you feel will help others. Because you have been placed in the lives of the parents you serve, it is important for you to bring your wisdom and skills to them too.

If you are interested in the skills that I tend to teach parents, they are laid out more fully in the omnibus edition of *Parenting Children for a Life of Faith*.[3] The website **parentingforfaith.org** is full of training videos, family stories and short articles that share skills and show what using those skills looks like in the lives of ordinary families. The website also has a free video-based Parenting for Faith course for individuals or groups to use. The course focuses on equipping parents in core skills.

Whether you use the core skills I have articulated in those books and on the website or develop your own, the more you give parents core skills in these four essential areas, the more they can grow in confidence and joy as they see their children flourish in their faith.

# This section

Part of our responsibility in enabling parents to parent for faith is to ensure that we are positioning ourselves to serve them well. It is important that we learn how to equip parents in a way that works best for them. The chapters in this section explore how we can impart skills to parents in a way that they can use quickly and competently, and see the fruit of their parenting for faith.

# 4

# Coaching a community

I remember the day I joined my school football team. The sign-ups opened one month into Year 5, and I was so excited. I loved playing football at breaks with my friends, and now I was going to join an official school team. I knew I was strong. I knew my friend Adam thought I was good. I was ready.

I was also very nervous. When I was in Year 4, I had watched the team practising and I saw how hard they worked warming-up, running drills and learning skills. I could see the coach took football very seriously. I knew if I were going to join this team, then I would be expected to work really hard; but I also knew the hard work was going to be so worth it because I would be learning so much. This coach was going to turn me into a proper football player.

Have you ever learned a sport? There are so many skills to learn that it is almost impossible for any athlete to become competent without a coach. It's a coach's job to equip athletes in those skills and to create a team environment in which the athletes work together as one.

I used to participate in a variety of sports throughout my childhood and teenage years, and I appreciated my coaches for stretching me and equipping me to do everything I wanted to do – even things I didn't know I could. They helped me grow in confidence through experience, mistakes and repetition. They let me try things I had no hope of doing on my own, and they supported me and caught me, so I didn't die. They inspired me, challenged me and journeyed with me, all in order to see me succeed.

We need to be like that for parents. We need to be the kind of excellent coaches who can help them pick up the vital skills they need to parent for faith effectively. And when parents become equipped with what they need, then that knowledge will transform them and their families. If we can do this well, significant changes will begin to occur.

## Coaching two levels

Sports coaches have to train their athletes on two levels at the same time: preparing the entire team as a group by teaching core skills, and preparing the individual by helping each one progress according to his or her needs and positions. The coach's ability to teach on both levels at the same time is what creates the most efficient process in which athletes can grow and develop.

Like sports coaches, we need to learn to teach parenting-for-faith skills on two levels. In this chapter, we will be looking at how to teach parents and extended families as a group. The next chapter will explore how we tailor and equip individuals on their unique journeys.

Let's look at six aspects of sports team-coaching and see what we can apply to our approach in coaching our parents in groups.

## Coach the ones who want it

Many times, we try to give skills to parents and extended families who haven't asked for them. Their lack of interest and cooperation can feel demoralising for us as leaders, as well as frustrating for them. A sports coach trains people who actively want to learn. We can be much more efficient if we focus on giving skills to the parents, carers and extended family who want to learn more and be better. Those who haven't indicated an interest are still 'envisioning', being exposed to our Ikea approach, being surrounded by the truths we are speaking and hearing stories that intrigue and inspire them. That is good enough. We've got to allow people to go on their own journeys. When they are ready to be coached, we can be there with open arms.

## Coach through consistency in relationship

Like it or not, the dynamic between the coach and the team is crucial to how well the athletes are going to pick up core skills. If the team members feel seen, loved, cared for and empowered, they will learn better. If they feel their coach is for them, with them and cheering them on, they will be freer to be bold without anxiety or fear.

For us to effectively teach core skills to parents, we need to choose to enter into a conscious relationship with those who attend our group events. We must maintain a *consistent* presence in their lives. This is key.

When we are consistent, we can get to know parents and their children. We become aware of their fears and strengths, and we learn how they interact as a group. We discover what stories help them, and who gets bored, and when. I have run the Parenting for Faith course for years, and I've found that every course has a different feel to it because each group of people is unique and their needs are slightly different. I know that I must get to know the group well enough to adjust my coaching to serve them best. Your relationship with a group is vital in helping you coach them well and in enabling them to learn skills together.

## Breaking down and building up the core skills

Diving is a good example of a sport where difficult moves consist of combinations of well-executed core skills. We have all watched in awe at high-divers flipping and twisting from the ten-metre board and entering the water with the splash of a tiny pebble. But in the beginning, divers didn't set out to learn that. No eight-year-old shows up to the first day of diving lessons to hear the coach say, 'Right. We are starting with a quadruple back somersault from a handstand off the ten metre. Let's get up there! I'll talk you through it!'

Before prospective divers can attempt any dive, the coach must first make sure they know the core basics: how to swim, how to jump and how to enter the water. Over and over, the coach has divers practise those core skills until they are second nature. Then, the coach leads them on to harder core skills: how to shape their bodies in the air and how to align themselves so they won't belly flop. As the coach strengthens and builds up the divers' core skills, they also help them combine those skills to form progressively more complex ones. For example, a diver will learn to complete their first dive from the side of the pool, then one from the board, and then one from the board adding a twist to the beginning. An effective coach knows that any big skill combination must first be broken down into its core elements; only then can the coach teach what is vitally necessary first, and later proceed to helping divers put those skills together into something more complex.

It is the same with parenting. Parents often come in thinking about the big 'quadruple back dive' skills and feel overwhelmed. How do I get my teenager to stop partying and love church again? How do I talk to my kid about God in the middle of my divorce? How do I help my dyslexic child love the Bible? The answer is that parents first need to learn a basic set of core skills which they can apply to most circumstances. We as coaches can teach parents and extended families the core skills, and we can help them build and strengthen those skills until they become second nature. We can then assist them in figuring out how to put those core skills together to conquer the big questions they have.

The role of a coach is to know what those core skills are and how to help parents become confident in them. There are some core skills that I feel are important for parents to have, which are included in the Parenting for Faith books mentioned above. Parents learn these skills and then combine them to tackle the large challenges of growing their children in faith, purpose and confidence.

You may have a different set of key skills that you want to give parents. Whatever you want to give them, I encourage you to break it down into core skills that parents can learn and then apply to bigger problems.

## Teach the whys, not just the whats

Sports coaches are so knowledgeable about everything they teach. They know small details like the correct angle of how hips should be aligned and which muscles to use and when. Because of their vast knowledge, they can give athletes quite specific instructions about *what* to do: 'Place your foot farther left from the ball.' What's more important, however, is that sports coaches also know the *whys* behind every skill they teach, and they're convinced that for players to truly pick up a skill and apply it well, they need to know the why behind how it works: 'By planting your foot on the side over here, it directs all your force forward, rather than in trying to keep your balance while swinging sideways. Driving forward makes your kick stronger.' Once players can understand why techniques work, they can begin to apply them wisely and adjust them to meet their changing situations.

When we try to encourage parents to take on new skills, we often fall into the trap of stating what *works* for children: 'For prayer with under-fives, we go around the circle and whisper to God out loud at church. You could try that at home. They love it.' But if we focused on explaining the *why* as well, parents could better implement the activity: 'When children are under five, they struggle to have an independent thought life that they are consciously aware of. This reality means that they use their external words and actions as part of their internal spiritual process. Praying out loud when talking to God helps them because it enables them to track their thoughts. Older children don't need this. But, to reinforce that their relationship with God is private, you can encourage them to whisper into their hands or a pillow. This helps their brains live their internal life out loud, while still encouraging them to have their personal and private connection with God.'

When we teach the whys, parents not only apply skills better, but they begin to experiment with them in different situations.

## The coach is the teacher and facilitator

Team members often learn from each other. They watch each other's progress and see how each other self-adjusts. They hear the coach working with individuals and apply that learning to themselves, and often they share struggles and adjustments with each other. Occasionally, they will approach each other and ask, 'Can you help me with this?'

But rarely are team members encouraged to wander up to each other and say, 'Let me teach you how to do it right.' That is the coach's job. There is safety in the coach being the one who provides instruction and helps the group and individuals grow. The coach's leadership allows everyone to be on a learning journey together and on an equal standing.

In parenting courses and at parenting events, to enable people's voices to be heard, we can accidentally allow active individuals to position themselves as occasional coaches, which can make people feel unsafe. As a coach, we can facilitate an excellent culture of story-sharing and mutual learning without allowing members of the group to step into proactive teaching roles that can put people off and destroy the safe dynamic in the room.

## Pastoral heart and the holistic approach

Coaches find it difficult to limit themselves to coaching only the athletic side of their players, because they know people are integrated beings. Sometimes a player's personal situation will affect their performance, and coaches can find themselves wading into that part of the athlete's life. Once a coach establishes trust with an athlete, that trust often will extend into other areas of the athlete's life. Coaches don't just help an athlete learn tennis, but also self-confidence, perseverance, how to cope with failure and more.

Often when coaching parents, we will get drawn into the wider lives of the people we serve. Marriage issues regularly come up, as well as general parenting hurts, fears about drugs or friends, frustrations with extended family, and old pain from abuse or disconnection. Be prepared for it. Often it happens in front of everyone. My general rule is that if parents are bold enough to bring up personal problems in front of everyone, then they deserve to be honoured, encouraged and affirmed in the same context. If we feel we can help, then we do. If we feel we have nothing to offer, then we can listen well and together with them think through the next steps that could link them to someone who can help. We can then keep following up with them to see how they are doing.

When we enter into equipping people to parent for faith, we walk into the deeply personal and vulnerable parts of their lives. It is a privilege we can steward well.

As we enable group members to learn core skills alongside each other, we build a 'team' community in which everyone supports each other with a sense of love, vulnerability and hope. It is a great privilege to coach parents and their communities in this way.

# 5

# Coaching individuals

Coaches don't just teach a skill to their team and then walk away. They stay with their athletes and help them take that skill and apply it to their own unique body types, personalities and roles. What can we learn from sports coaches that will enable us better to walk alongside parents as they grow in their skills? We can learn these five coaching tips.

## Let them learn through their attempts, failures, successes and adjustments

A coach knows athletes bring more than just their bodies to sports practice. They also bring their strengths, weaknesses, preferences, aches and pains, and life experiences. How one athlete integrates a new skill will be different from how the next athlete integrates it. Because the coach understands that acquiring a skill isn't as simple as just watching and doing it, they run their athletes through drills so they can repeatedly try and fail, adjust, and eventually integrate that skill into their lives in ways that work for them.

For us as leaders, the same principles apply. Parents and extended family members will each have their unique fears, family circumstances and experiences. Our job is not only to teach them core skills, but to be coaches who cheer them on and encourage them as they figure out how those skills work best in their family. Parenting is a learning journey. Don't be discouraged if those you work with take a while to pick up and use the skills effectively and easily. It takes practice.

When we teach core skills, we need to be aware that some parents may need help in adapting them for their particular family. They may have a partner who isn't a Christian, children who hate talking about emotions, or any one of a myriad of household scenarios. We can help them find a way to apply those core skills to their unique circumstances so that they can see their children and teens grow in God-connection.

## Build on their strengths

Every person is different, so the best coaches quickly assess each athlete's strengths and then build on those. All parents and extended families have natural parenting strengths, ways in which they may already be parenting for faith well. Our task is to find those strengths and build on them.

We can be so excited about equipping and encouraging parents that we accidentally communicate an enthusiastic 'Let me teach you something new!' This can come across as, 'You parents are clueless and starting from scratch. Let me teach you something that obviously is brand new to you!'

We need to shift our mindset to thinking, 'I'm just here to help your strengths get stronger, help you learn skills that you want to know, and give you a space to progress in the areas that are most important to you.' This communicates to parents and their support network that we are there to join them on their current journey, and to add momentum and additional skills to what they are already doing.

Another reason we look for and encourage strengths is because parents and extended family often really struggle to see how their current strengths translate into parenting for faith. I have known parents who are excellent at explaining life to their children, but they tell me that they don't know how to talk to their kids about God. It is so encouraging for me to say:

Well, I have seen you multiple times explain to your child about his dyslexia. You do that so well. You have given him a consistent framework in which to understand his experience, and you have explained to him how and why his brain works like that. Most importantly, you have shown him how to powerfully respond to his dyslexia needs. Those are the same skills we are talking about here. You can talk to your child about God in the same way you talk to him about dyslexia. Let me give you a few examples. Maybe when you pray before bed, you can pause and explain to your child how you feel when you connect with God and what God does when you pray. Maybe when you are driving and you see an accident, you can explain to him what is happening in your heart between you and God, and explain where God is in that moment. You already explain things well to your child; now it's just a matter of expanding what the topics are.

When parents already excel at explaining, storytelling or empowering their children to make choices, as coaches we can identify those strengths and build upon them.

The more we can positively affirm the strengths parents have, the more they can see how little tweaking it takes to parent for faith well. The more we know parents' strengths, the more we can be that truth-speaker and encourager in their lives.

## Let them learn at their own pace

A coach's job is to encourage, support and equip athletes to improve and progress. Some athletes learn skills quickly; others may take a long time to learn even one. Those differences are normal and to be celebrated. For us, the ease of equipping people to parent for faith is that no matter what pace they want to go at, we can always be there to help them.

Recently I was in an exercise class and was not coping well. At all. I was gasping and sweating and gulping water and not keeping up. The trainer would show a move, and the other 20 people in the room would shuffle a bit and try it. He'd call out, 'Weight under your chin, left leg back, front leg lunged, and dip!' And everyone looked fine – except for me. I could barely find the position, much less bounce like he wanted me to. I was on the verge of giving up.

But the trainer saw I needed help. He continued leading the skill from the front of the room, but he began to call out possible adjustments. 'If you are struggling with this position, bring your left leg back in so you're just sitting in the air on two bent legs and then bounce.' I adjusted, as did a few others. While that new position was easier for me, I still couldn't do it. Other people around me continued on, having no problem with the original skill.

He noticed me again and called out, 'If anyone is struggling with the two-leg position, just put the weight down. The important thing is to work those thighs.' I dropped that weight like a sack of potatoes, and I felt instant relief. While everyone else kept bouncing away, I settled for merely moving up and down slowly.

After class, the trainer came back to encourage me. He told me to do only what I felt I could do confidently, and as I got stronger I would be able to do the skills better.

Many times parents feel pushed into needing to do things they feel ill-equipped to do. What we can do is slow that down, and make sure they are implementing skills they feel completely prepared to do. I spend a lot of my ministry saying to parents, 'Don't worry about that next bit yet. Do this bit well now, and it will have a huge impact on your child. This is enough for now! Get this bit to where you are comfortable with it, and then when you are ready to add a new skill, you can. You've got it!'

# Praise their progress and the effort

Coaches exist to help athletes improve and progress, and to champion their efforts and successes along the way. The other day I was watching a child's tennis class. All the children were lined up taking turns at returning the ball over the net. But there was one student who was really struggling. He just couldn't manage to coordinate his arms with the rest of his body. The ball always seemed to zoom past him before he could run to it and swing his racquet. Again and again his turn would come, and again and again he would miss. The coach continued to give him encouragement and instructions each and every time he tried.

And then it happened. The boy arrived at the front of the queue, the tennis ball was lobbed towards him and, using all the effort he had, he lunged and his racquet connected with the ball. Wham! The ball spun off to the side, nowhere near the court, but the coach shouted with joy and ran towards the beaming boy. They jumped and high-fived and together celebrated his achievement. The goal of successfully returning the ball over the net was a long way away. But the little goal of progress was a great triumph of effort and perseverance, and it deserved to be celebrated.

Often when we coach parents, we can see the ones who pick up skills right away and the ones who need a lot more practice. Once I worked with a dad who struggled with anger. He came in one day to tell me a story about something that happened in his week. Evidently, when he and his daughter were outside, there was a moment when he thought she was going to run into the road (she wasn't). The dad lost his temper, yelled at her and called her stupid.

Tears filled his eyes as he told me that when he kissed his daughter before she went to bed, he apologised to her for yelling. It was the first time he had ever apologised to her for that. He told her that he didn't do a good job of keeping his heart close to God's peace. He was scared when he thought she was running into the road and he responded in a way that wasn't like God's heart. He told his daughter how sorry he was. He let her know he had spent some time with God asking his forgiveness and figuring out what was going wrong with his heart. And now he wanted to ask his daughter's forgiveness. The dad addressed how untrue the word 'stupid' was, and he spoke of all the wonderful things he saw in his daughter. They hugged and cried, and then tickled and laughed.

This dad was so, so proud of himself. His connection with his daughter was better than ever. Is this an ideal story? No. Ideally he would not have yelled at his daughter or called her names. But as a coach, I watched this man go from having a general disconnection with his daughter to being able to talk with her about a mistake he had made in a way that also showed a bit of God's heart and what life with God looked like. I was over the moon.

When we celebrate progress, no matter how small, then parents and extended families see us as in their corner, witnessing the triumphs of life with them.


## Be an 'outside eye'

When I was nine years old I did gymnastics, and I would rely on my coach to see the things I couldn't see. Usually I could assess for myself what I was doing wrong. If I missed the asymmetric bar, I knew it was because I didn't push hard enough. If I slammed my knees on the vault, I knew I needed to lift my bum higher. But there were many times I didn't understand what I was doing wrong.

During one practice session I was consistently landing on my knees and my face when I tried to do a somersault. I knew I needed to go faster, but what did I need to adjust? Was it that I didn't jump high enough? Or that I didn't pull my knees in tight enough or fast enough? Or was it that I wasn't leaning back at the right angle when I jumped? Since my coach was helping someone else, I chose to guess and make my own adjustments. I ended up exhausted and wondering if I would ever get it right.

But then my coach came over and said, 'Show me.' One more time I tried and crashed. 'It's your arms,' he said, before I could even get up. 'Lean, jump, *up arms*, snap! You are just going: lean, jump, snap! And so your only momentum is the force of your head.'

So I tried it again, this time focusing on my arms, and I landed perfectly. I needed that 'outside eye', because my body didn't quite have everything memorised yet. With one glance, he pointed out what was holding me back.

We can serve as 'outside eyes' for parents. As they grow in their skills, we can come with a different perspective to help spot something that is making them frustrated. When parents feel they're at a brick wall, they often don't need to relearn everything; they just need one insight that helps them find the next step.

It takes discipline to restrain ourselves from trying to teach them everything all over again. When we hold ourselves to just focusing on helping them break down the wall, trusting that they can take the next steps on their own, they feel hugely empowered:

> Hmm, that isn't unusual, Lydia. Other people have found that their children don't think primarily in pictures either. You may want to try a different way for them to have a conversation with God. When your child really wants to tell you something important, what does she do? Ooh, interesting. Well, I would suggest you try helping your child communicate with God that way. Do you think that might help?

Sometimes parents just need a crash course in something new. I have taught many skills in a mini-version format while standing in the corner of a church because a parent needed to know how to answer tough questions or how to help a child with ADHD chat with God. Our role is to equip their next steps so they don't ever feel they're stuck or at a dead end.

When we choose to be like sports coaches, imparting skills both in a group and individually, we can ensure all parents and carers are gaining what they need to see their children and teens connect with God.

# 6

# Being a help desk

The wind was up. I live in North Yorkshire, God's own county (take that, Lancashire), and the wind is a character all to itself. Sometimes it is chaotic, sometimes gentle. Sometimes it spits on you while it blows, or whips around you in a way that makes no sense. One day it was mad at something and was pushing trees over. The problem was that I desperately needed to get to London. Evidently, though, trains have to tiptoe through strong wind, and our little train travelled so slowly that I missed my connection.

Usually I would just jump on the next train, but the board was full of delays and cancellations. I was frustrated and not sure what to do. My brain was spinning with questions. What kind of ticket did I have? Which train line could I travel on? Should I wait for my delayed train, or get my ticket reissued for a later one?

Then, a shining booth seemed to emerge out of the sea of rushing people: the help desk. A choir sang in my head. Yes! The help desk! I bumped through the crowd and edged my way into the queue. All hell was breaking loose in Leeds station, but inside the help desk booth, people looked calm and casual, as if it were a day at the park.

I watched in awe as the help desk personnel rattled off train schedules from memory, sketched out plans for people by hand, and calculated train platforms *in their heads*. By the time I got to the front of the queue, I was supremely peaceful. I still had no idea how to get anywhere, but I was confident I would know in three minutes. I would be told.

'Can I help you?' asked the smiling, uniformed woman behind the counter. When she leaned forward a bit, I could read her name tag: Priya.

'Yes, please,' I answered. 'I need to get to London. I have a single advance ticket, and I don't know where to go.'

'Okay. What time do you need to get there? And would a particular station be useful?'

'Oh! I need to be at Seven Sisters at 11.40. I was thinking about just getting on the next train to London.'

'Well, you certainly could do that. Let me see if I can make it better for you. Hmm…' I watched Priya's brain calculate as she stared off into space. Soon she looked back at me and smiled again. 'Well, you can take this next train that's going there with stops. It will be very slow, and there is a chance they will cancel it. The one in an hour is a direct train. It may be delayed getting here, but once it is here, it should be fine. But again, the weather is unpredictable. I think it will miss your target time, though, but it won't be too far off. Or you can get adventurous and do the cross country to Birmingham and then to London, which bizarrely will get you there on time, but it takes two hours longer than the other trains. It all depends on what you want.'

My jaw dropped. I made my choice, and Priya fixed my ticket. I was on my way to Platform 3. A few minutes later I saw her as I walked past the help desk on my way to the toilet. 'Did you find the right platform?' she called. I felt so special. The help desk lady noticed me! 'Yes! I'm just popping to the loo!' She nodded and waved. Twenty minutes later, I boarded my train, saw a bit of Birmingham, and made it to my meeting in London by the skin of my teeth. I couldn't believe the difference the help desk made in my life that day. I went from frantic and frustrated to peaceful and empowered in three minutes.

Once parents identify someone who can equip them and help them, they begin to feel free to ask questions. And asking questions isn't bad. It's an excellent sign. It means they are engaged and thinking about their parenting. It means they see you as someone who cares, who's on their side and who doesn't judge them. It's great.

But how we choose to respond to these questions can make a tremendous impact on parents. We can respond in a way that empowers and encourages, or we can respond in a way that leaves them feeling less confident and more reliant on us.

So, what are the keys to positioning ourselves to answer questions in a way that causes parents to flourish? I suggest we begin to think of ourselves as a help desk. There are a few things we can learn from Priya.

## Be available

In the train station, I went to the help desk primarily because it was available and glowing in front of me. Now, I know this may sound silly, but in the rush of Sunday mornings or normal life, we sometimes are pretty hard to get a hold of for casual conversations. The key here is the word 'casual'. Rarely do parents feel their question is important enough to make a phone call or to send an email asking for advice. Even though their problem may be quite significant, they may hold on to it for a long time – unless they can easily find us.

The head teacher at my son's school stands near the front gates every day, rain or shine, for the ten minutes before school and after school. It is awesome. Sometimes I happily join the queue to ask her a question. She either answers it there or she makes a note to get in contact with me later. And then she does. It is fantastic. In most churches I've been in, I try to do the same. I pick a spot in the main area where I can plant myself for a good chunk of time, allowing parents to bump into me or grab me for a quick question.

Where can we put ourselves so that we can be available for those casual conversations? So the parents we serve can say to a friend, 'I'll be right back. I want to ask something,' and then can find us quickly without chasing us through corridors?

## Listen well

When I was stuck in Leeds station, Priya asked me a series of questions to understand my situation before she gave me an answer. She could have just pointed to the next train to London, but she took the time to understand my circumstance, which meant that she helped me find a much better way forward.

When parents ask us a question, we also need to understand their circumstance. We figure that out by asking questions. When we do, we often run into much bigger situations than the one they initially presented.

'How do I help my kid with nightmares?' seems like a simple question parents ask. I could happily suggest some ways forward, focusing around the subject of fear and bedtime. But if I take the time to ask questions to understand more about their circumstances, then I can be sure the help I give will be the most relevant. I'll often reply to a parent's question with something like, 'Oh no, what has been going on?' This opens up the conversation, and then they tell me the whole story. I'll continue by asking follow-up questions: Are the nightmares repetitive? Are they one-offs? How are you coping with it so far? What have you tried? What has been helpful?

When we listen well, we can make sure we aren't functioning like an internet search engine, just spitting out the most likely answers to the questions that appear.

When I am listening to parents tell me their story, I usually ask myself one question: what is the fear behind this story? Sometimes parents' questions are straightforward, but often their questions hide deeper concerns that they haven't expressed yet. They could be fearful that if God doesn't stop the nightmares, then their child will think God doesn't exist. Or they might be worried that if they don't give good enough answers about God, then their child will stop trusting them as parents. As I talk with parents and carers, I try to sense if there is fear that I also need to be aware of and address. If I am able to ask, 'How is this impacting your child's connection with God?', then parents have space to voice those fears and to feel like you are on their team.

As help-desk people, our first job is to fully understand, and then to craft our answers to respond to, both the immediate need and the underlying fears.

## Praise what you can

When I talked to Priya, I told her my solution to my problem, and she immediately confirmed to me that my solution was valid. Part of me was so relieved that I wasn't as lost as I thought. But she didn't just pat me on the back and let me go. She had a much better solution for me.

When dealing with parents' questions, so often our minds instantly go into problem-solving mode. 'I have the answer,' we think. But first we need to pause. Our job as encouragers of parents is always to reinforce the essential truths we want them to know: they are the experts in their children; they already are doing many things well; there is not only one right way to handle the situation.

Before we give our answers it is constructive for us to encourage parents in what they already have been doing. Sometimes in the process of hearing more about the situation, parents will tell us their journey of how they've been trying to help their child so far. In that case, we can affirm what they have been doing. 'I can see why you went with that first; it would have been my first suggestion too. I can see why you are frustrated.' Or, 'Oh, that's a really good idea. It's so creative. I can imagine Sam would have liked that.' Or, 'Well, that was definitely worth a try.'

If we don't know the parents' journey, then we can feel free to ask, 'What have you tried and how did it go?' This not only helps us to better understand the need, but it also communicates to parents and carers that we assume they've already tried things. If they haven't tried anything yet, we can affirm them by saying, 'That's totally okay! I'm here to help you think through stuff.'

When parents put a problem on the table and we join them midway through the process, they feel less like they are under scrutiny. They can see we recognise that their problem is tricky and has a lot of variables and that we are only a part of their next steps. We join their team in figuring out how to help their child. We aren't the experts taking over their parenting job because they had to escalate the need to us.

## Give choices

When parents ask us questions, one of the biggest temptations is to respond with our best answer. It makes sense. Often parents or carers will ask us for a specific, definitive answer about what they should do, and we usually have a clear opinion so we are happy to give it to them. My main advice is this: don't do it.

Stick with me here. When I finally got to the Leeds station help desk, I wanted Priya to tell me exactly what to do. I wanted her to take away all the choices that were drowning me and just hand me the answer. She didn't do that. Instead, she simplified the options to just the ones that would give me what I needed, and she let me choose what I thought worked best for me.

We have to keep our eye on the goal. The goal isn't to solve problems for the parents; the goal is to help parents solve problems for themselves.

In the end, we are here to help parents take the next steps, to give them lots of paths that can lead them to the ultimate goal, and to enable them to look at the choices and decide what is right for their child in this circumstance. If one doesn't work, they can try the others. If they don't choose any, we still have helped expand their understanding of the issue and stirred their minds to consider other ways to solve the problem. By giving them a range of options, we are showing them that we are on their team and that there is no one right way of handling this issue. There are several wise ways forward, and we trust they will be able to find the right one for them.

So, don't give your opinion. Don't tell them what to do.

Instead, *always* give them a choice. Provide them with a range of options. You may be 100% convinced that there is a clear right way forward for this child. Tough. Create choices anyway.

This requires us to have an enormous amount of self-control and to constantly reposition our hearts to focus on empowering parents. Because when we do, we grow parents who are always learning and becoming better and who are growing in confidence in their ability to learn while doing.

Giving choices doesn't mean that we give wishy-washy answers or hide solid advice. It means that we are rigorous to present a series of good options to show them the range of what they can do, regardless of which one we think is best.

Giving choices applies even to simple questions. 'Which Bible should I buy my kid?' was a common question I would get in my first children's pastor job. I had a straightforward answer, which obviously was going to be the Bible I bought for the entire children's ministry. I also had a myriad of reasons why I chose that Bible. Everything in me wanted to say, 'This one!' Instead, I would swallow my opinion and tell them:

> Well, it really depends on what you are looking for. Which kid is it for? Why now? What are you hoping will happen? What have you tried so far? How is she engaging with that? Hmm, interesting. Well, Bible A has good sentence structure and is suitable for early readers, so that may be helpful if one of your main concerns is ease of reading. But if you are looking for something more substantial, Bible B has a good concordance and little inserts of cool themed Bible studies which can help children feel more confident in navigating the Bible and applying it to themselves. Bible C is a lot more impressive to look at and read, which some children find allows them to read for longer. Unfortunately, it doesn't have inserts or any cross-referencing, but not every child needs that. They are all equally good choices. Which do you think would work best for Gracie?

If we don't know the choices that are out there, we can always say:

> Interesting! I'll have a look around and find out what other kids are using and get back to you with some options. We use this Bible at church, but I'm sure there are other great options out there too. Let me find some choices for you.

When we give choices, we acknowledge that their child or teen is unique and there are lots of positive ways forward. We communicate that we are here to help them choose what they think is right.

## Follow-up

When Priya saw me walking away from my platform to the loo, she called out to check that I was okay and knew what I was doing. I was so happy to be noticed and felt so safe that no matter what happened, I knew I had a partner in the help desk. Her little moment of follow-up made me feel I wasn't on my own.

It is a small thing to remember to follow-up with parents, yet the impact on them can be significant. When we send a simple email or text or have a chance encounter with a parent and ask about their progress, they can feel so cared for and served.

> I was just thinking about you today. Did you ever manage to find a Bible for your daughter? How is it going? What did you choose in the end?

> How is Grandma doing? What did you decide about how to tell Johnny? How do you feel about it? Is there anything I can do to help you as you parent through this tough season?

A quick follow-up connection tells parents that you aren't just an opinion machine. It shows them that you care about them and the development of their children, and you are interested in how it's going. It makes them feel seen.

It also gives an excellent opportunity to encourage them:

> Oh, interesting! I hadn't even thought of that Bible, but you are right, that combines application with Manga style. Glad it's helping. Would you recommend it for others? I'll put that in my back pocket in case I hear of any other parents on the trawl.

> Sounds like you handled that beautifully. I'm so glad you were on it. It looks like your kid is flourishing in this season. Go you.

## The proactive help desk

On the day of the big windstorm, the station brought in extra people to work with the help desk. Their job was to wander around and approach lost and frustrated people and ask them if they needed help. It was incredible to watch these uniformed workers bring calm to so many flustered commuters.

Sometimes parents are overwhelmed and don't know you are there to help. Sometimes they will need us to wade in. That is also one of our roles: to walk into people's fear and frustration and ask if they need help.

There are many times when I have had to grab a dad and ask:

> How are your kids doing spiritually with your wife's cancer? That can't be easy to coach them through it. You aren't alone. How are you doing with it? How can I help you with your kids? Would you like me to babysit your young ones so you can have one-to-one time to talk with your oldest about it? How can I be with you as you and your wife make this awful journey with your kids?

When we get this right, we don't come in saying, 'You need to do this, and I will tell you how.' We come in saying, 'This looks tough, and I've got your back. You've got this, and I'm here if you need help.'

## Handling the pressure

There are so many times we can feel inadequate when we support parents. We can feel we aren't smart enough, experienced enough or wise enough to help. I know some of us feel we shouldn't have a voice in the lives of parents because we don't have children.

You will find that most parents don't care.

When I spoke with Priya at the station help desk, not once did I think, 'How often has she travelled on trains? Is she the most experienced train traveller here?' I wasn't looking to her for an answer from her own experience. I was looking to her as the person who had put herself there to help me. I trusted that she would help. If she knew the answer, she would give it. If she didn't, she would find it. She was committed to helping me, and that was what I needed.

When I was a 26-year-old children's pastor, people would be asking me parenting advice for their 17-year-old boy. Not because I had parented a 17-year-old boy before, but because I was a youth worker who had served a lot of parents over the years and had access to knowledge they needed. They knew I loved them and loved their son, and they knew I would help them to the best of my ability. That was what they needed.

We do a disservice to parents, carers and extended families if we limit our answers to just our own wisdom and experience. I am a parent, but my goal is not for parents to look at my parenting and do what I do. Their children are different from my child. Their circumstances are different from mine. When I answer a question, I'm not thinking, 'What would I do?' I'm thinking, 'Based on all the parents I've worked with, the books and research I've read, my experience in working with children across the years, and the wise people I know, here are some of the options that might work for you.'

There will be times when we don't know the answers. That is okay. There may be times when we need to go pioneer some solutions. We may need to do some research, or even sit with some children and find out what works best. We are all on the journey of learning more, and there will be times when your knowledge runs out. It is part of your job to sometimes have to say, 'I don't know yet, but I'll figure it out. Or find someone who can help.'

When we choose to serve parents in this manner, we realise that it isn't about us being the smartest or wisest people in the room. It is about us choosing to be the help desk, enabling parents to see the array of choices they have and to continue confidently on their journey of parenting.

# Church
# culture

# Introduction:
# an integrated plan

God has designed an integrated plan, a blended system, in which children and young people can grow a lifelong relationship with him. Parents are a central component of that plan, but they aren't the only component in the mix.

Think of it like tea.

What makes an excellent cup of tea? It isn't simply about which brand you like best. While tea leaves are a crucial ingredient, they aren't the only part. There is a myriad of factors that go into making a wonderful cup of tea: the temperature of the water, how long it is steeped, the amount and timing of the milk, the kind and amount of sugar used, and even the choice of a favourite mug. It is the integration of all the factors that makes the perfect cuppa.

Similarly, for discipling children, God has designed an integrated network of parents, extended family and friends, congregations and local church leaders who together create a blended culture in which children and teens can grow in their connection with God.

# Parents

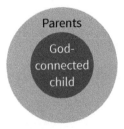

As we have seen in Deuteronomy 6:4–9, God has centred children's discipleship in the relationships that govern their everyday lives. This kind of discipleship occurs in the daily humdrum of life, because within repetitive normalness there is time for reality with God to grow. That is the space where faith and reality can meet and be experienced.

Whoever is positioned in the child's life to provide the parenting love, guidance and safety is the best person to help the child connect with God, whether that provider is a natural or adoptive parent, carer or grandparent. These parents and carers are the ones who can weave faith in as part of the reality of life rather than as an optional add-on. They can show how God is present and accessible even in the simplicity of familiar routines.

The Bible is full of parents and carers who discipled the children in their care. Eunice, Timothy's mother, raised him in an environment where he grew to know and love God (2 Timothy 1:5). Eli, who cared for Samuel, helped him recognise the voice of God (1 Samuel 3).

Even though those who function in a parental role are naturally the primary disciplers of their children, they were never meant to do it alone. Parents were not meant to be isolated from the other rings of support in God's design.

# Extended family and friends

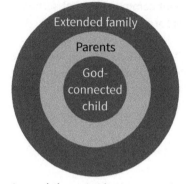

Around those in the parent role, God has placed extended family, friends and tight-knit communities to support children and to embrace, equip and support parents. Scripture calls them *oikos* or households of faith.[4] These are grandparents, godparents, close friends, small groups and other Christian parents.

These people are vital to the spiritual development of children and teens. They give children a community to see themselves in, access to other God stories and a safe place to learn what life with God looks like for people outside their immediate family.

In the Bible, we see Timothy growing into a church leader through this investment of the extended family and tight-knit community around him and his mother, Eunice. Timothy's grandmother Lois was significant in his life, too, and even the apostle Paul chose to mentor Timothy, opening opportunities for the young man to minister.

When parents have a solid network of extended family and friends, they have people to laugh with, share stories with and get advice from. They watch other people help their children with God and they learn how to do it well themselves. As they gain experience, they begin to mentor other families, yet they still benefit from the blessing of being mentored and encouraged themselves. If we are going to see God-connected young people grow, we not only have to equip parents, but also strengthen, train, encourage and embolden the extended family, friends and tight-knit communities that surround them – whether or not they are a part of our congregations.

But the layers of integration don't stop there. While parents are discipling their children, and their extended family are providing input, the church provides these families with an outer ring of support.

## Church

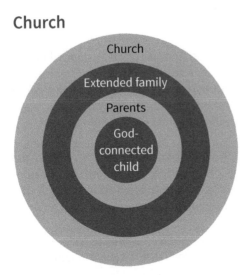

A church is significant in two different ways. First, it creates a space for children to learn how to be fully functioning members of the body of Christ, and to feel what it's like to be side by side with people of all ages walking life with God together in worship and mission. It can provide a peer group to learn with, as well as provide access to seeing new things of God through church activities.

Often in the Bible, when large groups gathered together for significant purposes, children were present alongside the adults. Children were there on the hillsides when Jesus taught, and sometimes people brought them to Jesus (Matthew 19:13–14). Children were among the crowds in Galilee, and participated in the feeding of the 5,000 (John 6:9); they saw and experienced that miracle for themselves. Children were part of the multitude who stood before God in expectation as King Jehoshaphat prayed for help in the face of near-certain death (2 Chronicles 20:13) and among those who assembled to listen to Ezra read the Book of the Law and who wept as they understood its meaning (Nehemiah 8:2–3, 9). Children witnessed the miracles of the exodus and witnessed the healing power of Jesus the Messiah. Throughout the Bible, children experienced God in significant ways when they were a part of a large multigenerational assembly of believers who were seeking and following God.

Second, the church establishes a culture in which families can flourish. Church communities dedicate themselves to helping people learn how to live in the fullness of Christ. Often parents have come from non-faith backgrounds or faith backgrounds that pushed them away; they may have no idea how to live in the fullness of Christ. But God has placed them in our churches so that they can learn to be who they are called to be in Christ, and then they can develop the inspiration, values and skills to parent their own children to connect with God and for a lifelong journey with him.

I often think back to the early church. I love when Paul writes to the Ephesians and specifically addresses the children and parents he knew would be in the room when his letter was read publicly. These Ephesian parents were learning about God and trying to figure out how to parent for faith at the same time, and the larger church community was supporting them.

God's best for our children is when parents and extended families are embedded in a church that embraces the power it has in creating a culture where parenting for faith can flourish. The church has so much to give parents and extended families: access to a wide community of believers, structures that equip and strengthen their role in their families, opportunities to learn and experiment, and wholehearted encouragement and leadership in introducing new ideas and skills.

Parents cannot do their job alone. But when we as a church wrap ourselves around them and their extended families and friends with our love and effort, then God's discipleship plan for children and young people functions fully.

The following chapters look at how we can adjust our church structures and approaches to deliberately create a culture where parenting for faith flourishes, self-replicates and grows organically.

# 7

# Creating space for skills to grow

I'm going to make a confession: I once got caught for speeding. As it was a first offence, the gracious British government decided to offer me mercy. They gave me a choice: take three points on my licence or go on a speed-awareness course. I could take an entire day away to learn about my wayward ways, gain a vision for an alternative life of lawfulness and learn the skills I so obviously needed to regulate my speed better.

It sounded as appealing as listening all day to a bunch of children learning recorders while also being repeatedly poked with a stick. But I did not want points on my licence, so I leapt at the opportunity.

The day arrived. I showed up and milled about with 35 other reluctant sinners. Many of them were bitter at being there and were planning on being as awkward as humanly possible for our poor teacher. I was still on my indignant high-horse as well. (Please – going 54 mph in a 50 mph zone hardly demands a day of remedial training, right?) Anyway, our valiant teacher, John, soon arrived clutching a stack of folders with papers falling out of them and murmuring about the tech not working. He was in his mid 40s, and his face was red from the effort of carrying his multiple boxes. We watched in silence and with a bit of righteous judgement while he set up, got his PowerPoint presentation running and settled in. I braced myself for the worst.

I can tell you now, over nine years on, that it was the best training day I have ever attended. I would 100% go again *for fun*. Our group actually groaned in disappointment when he insisted on breaking for lunch because we didn't want to stop. We even stayed 15 minutes after the end of the day because we had so many questions.

What made the day so remarkable? John showed us videos of massive car crashes and then paused for us to predict what would happen next (betting with sweeties). He drew lines on the board where people began to brake and then asked us to guess their speed. He had us conduct physics experiments to discover the reasons behind particular speed limits. He put on music and had us create Lego inventions to prove to us that we do things faster when we are upbeat or listening to exciting music. He had us do puzzles and maths while he made sounds in the background to show us how our ability to concentrate is compromised when we're distracted. At the end of the day, he gave us group quizzes that had us cackling with laughter, and then he showed us a video of people telling sad stories of losing their loved ones in speeding accidents, which brought us all to guilty tears. It was fantastic.

I left convinced about the value of speed control. It was bizarre. My husband was legitimately concerned. I came home bubbling with interesting statistics and with my behaviour adjusted. And I think I'm a better driver now because of what I learned on that day.

When I first arrived on the morning of the training day, I was expecting John to lecture me for seven hours, adding a few pictures into the mix. If he had done that, I'm sure I would have learned something, but only a little. John instead used a huge variety of techniques to teach me information and skills. And I retained most of it.

As churches, we have a unique opportunity to use as many creative techniques as we can to train and equip parents and extended families so the skills they learn will embed deeply within them. So often we think that means we just need to do what John did and become much more interactive during our teaching sessions. But that would be too limiting. Why? Because we are not limited to one day with parents and extended families. They don't just come to endure a one-off lecture. How much more creative can we be when we are a consistent presence in the lives of families over a long span of time? How much more can we coach those core skills when we weave together an Ikea-like series of opportunities to gain and exercise those skills? What if we really looked at the breadth and depth of how we can facilitate parents and carers to engage with ideas, learn and practise skills, and try new techniques as part of their everyday engagement with us as a church?

There are many creative ideas out there for creating spaces, many more than I can cover in this chapter. On our website **parentingforfaith.org**, we gather together stories from volunteers and church workers who have shared what they have been doing in their local churches. I firmly believe that you too will pioneer fantastic, creative ideas that I'd want to learn from and others would benefit from. For now, I just want to point you to a few general ways in which we can create space for parents' and extended families' skills to grow.

## Gathered teaching

When we teach, our default technique is to gather people together formally. It is an effective method of teaching, and when it comes to 'skilling-up' parents and carers in helping their children and teens connect with God, it is incredibly efficient. As an individual, it can be hard to gather people together in order to teach them something, but the church has the ability to easily facilitate a large gathering for an event such as a Parenting for Faith course.

### The course

I'm always looking for an opportunity to run the Parenting for Faith course.[5] Unlike most parenting courses, this one ultimately focuses on giving parents and extended families the core skills they need to help their children connect with God and develop their own life of faith. The course is most effective when church leaders creatively adapt it to fit the unique designs of their communities.

Too often we fall into the typical church mode of placing the course in the evening and advertising it as much as possible. But for some communities within our churches, that isn't the best time. Evenings can be difficult for many families, because it is hard to find childcare or they are too tired or busy to come.

Some churches prefer to arrange childcare to make it easier for the adults to attend. Several churches I know wanted to invest in the community aspect of the course, so they arranged for the course to happen after church. The families would all eat together and get to know each other's children, and when it was time for the course to begin, the church provided childcare. They also shortened each course session so that everyone would be home by 2.00 pm. As a result, these churches saw an increase in the attendance of both parents within families, solo parents, and youth and children's workers. They even saw families from other churches come to join in.

Other churches I know ran the course once a month during a Sunday-morning service. They figured families were already coming and their children were already attending activities, so the families would not be burdened with any additional requirements. This resulted in a very close-knit community, since they journeyed as a group for the better part of a year. In addition to the typical spread of parents, they also drew in a larger proportion of families with under-5s and a significant amount of extended families and people from the wider community. Aunts and uncles, godparents, grandparents and even family friends came.

Another church broke the course down even further into chunks and ran it for an entire year as an option alongside their morning tots groups. By spreading out the course's topics in this way, the church enabled not just Christian parents to come but also a large number of parents who were only vaguely interested in God. As a result, several people became Christians and the general faith interest of the group rose.

A few churches I know have also decided that the content is something that their whole congregation would benefit from, so they have used the course as the primary curriculum for their midweek home groups.

But the course isn't the only opportunity to impart skills in a formal, gathered way; it's just the most systematic one.

## One-off events

Another effective way that we can teach specific skills is through one-off events. Such events are great opportunities to teach those little, momentum-building skills that parents need and are designed to be short enough that we can quickly add them in whenever we see a need.

The key to the success of these events is in their specificity. Often, one-off sessions have vague topics, which makes them ineffective because they try to accomplish too much in a short time. As a result, parents don't feel the events are worth the effort to attend.

By designing an event around a specific topic, we can dig into the details of that topic and parents benefit more from the experience. For example, rather than having a 'young families' event, where we want people to 'be encouraged in the ups and downs of parenting under-fives' – which could mean anything – we could focus on a single concept or skill:

> **Young families' night of stories** – come for an informal night of sharing stories about the spiritual journeys of under-fives. Feel free just to come, listen and be encouraged! If you are willing, bring your own stories of your moments of 'epic

failures', lessons you have learned from others, glimpses of God-connections in your children or your surprising stories of 'well, that worked'. We'll spend the evening eating cake, laughing and encouraging each other.

**Connecting toddlers and babies to God in worship** – children can connect with God in worship at any age. Join us with your family on Sunday morning before church for some waffles and a short, practical workshop in how to help your children connect with God in worship. This workshop is applicable to worship in your home and in church services. We want you to feel hopeful and excited about worshipping side by side with each other as a young family.

One-off events can cover a range of topics, from how to coach children through news items, to how to coach your child through social media or how to maintain connection with your child when your work schedule keeps you away.

They also give us the opportunity to respond to a specific group of parents in a particular season of life. I'm currently looking at designing a one-off night to run after an Alpha course for new Christians. New Christians often find themselves trying to explain the change that has occurred within them to their children and wanting to add a new strand to their parenting that they have never considered before, while still feeling incredibly inexperienced. As it may be a while until the next Parenting for Faith course comes around, I'd love to give them a one-off night to encourage them in how to start straight away.

When we are specific, one-off events can be powerful places in which we can impart vision and skills to parents and extended families and help them leap forward in their ability to parent for faith successfully.

# The springboard resources

In the comedy movie *Hitch*, the title character helped awkward individuals get into the dating scene. Hitch's theory was that the awkward people just needed help to get past the agonising anxiety of the initial few dates so they could finally be themselves and see if the relationship would work. His rule was that he would help people until the third date or the first kiss, whichever came first, and then they were on their own.

When I first saw the film, I remember thinking, '*That's* what parents need. Parents need help getting past the agonising anxiety of starting. Once they get going, they can do it.'

I began to think about resources. What if I could create resources specifically for getting parents to overcome their inertia, but ones that still provided a lot of space for them to try out the new skills we've been teaching them? Even better, what if I could create resources that actually trained them in skills *as* they used them? The resources could be a springboard, enabling parents to do things they didn't think were initially possible.

Thus began many years of experimentation to create these 'springboard' resources. As I got better at making them, I began to notice a difference in parents. They began to love springboards. They looked for them and asked for them, and then, bizarrely, they stopped using them. New parents to the church would go on the same journey: try them, love them, seek them out and then drop them.

When I asked more experienced parents how I could make the resources better, they assured me the resources didn't need to be better; it was just that they didn't need them any more. They eventually felt confident enough to continue without them. Success, then, was in the resources becoming obsolete.

Springboards can be opportunities to teach parents the four core skills I mentioned in the introduction to Part 2, 'Skills'. The following are examples of how I used a springboard resource to teach the third core skill – how parents can proactively disciple their children.

One baptism Sunday, I noticed that many children were disengaged, and most parents spent their time chasing and disciplining their children. I felt that parents were desperate for a few skills on how to proactively disciple their children during a service, so I created a little springboard resource. I made a booklet with little pictures like app icons, which would serve as signposts throughout the service. At the side of every image were a few sentences explaining what was happening in that part of the service, and some suggestions for parents on what to draw their children's attention to. I made these booklets available to parents before the service. Then, during the service, I put up a picture of the icon on an easel at the front of the church. Whenever parents saw a new one, they would bend down and whisper to their children, and use the booklet to help their children know what was happening and to point out interesting things for them to notice or look out for.

At first, everyone was using the booklets. After a few services, I began to see that only new families were using the booklets, but that most of the other families were still bending down to remind their children what was happening. I also noticed that those same, experienced families continued to whisper to their children on Sundays, even when unprompted. Creating this springboard resource ended up equipping most parents and extended families in how to coach their children through a service, without me ever having to teach anything about it formally.

Another example of a springboard resource is an opportunity I created for fathers and daughters to talk with each other at a deeper, emotional level. I knew that an older man's voice was powerful in the life of a growing girl or teenager, and I wanted to help those connections grow. Some of the men already had these skills, but for others this was relatively new. I planned a father–daughter event that included plenty of activities that would ensure a lot of messiness, laughter, challenges and fun.

It turned out that dads weren't the only ones interested in attending; we also had stepfathers, uncles, godfathers, grandfathers, family friends and others. The rule was one man per child, in order to reinforce the one-to-one bond. We were very aware that in that room we had divorced fathers, men who were only allowed to see their children under supervision and some who were new to this relationship. We decided to call them 'teammates' to avoid confusion or awkwardness.

In talking with some of the men, I found that their chief anxiety in having emotional conversations with the girls in their lives was that they didn't know what to ask, and they didn't know what to share. So, I created a simple game that consisted of a stack of cards with questions on them for the girls to ask the men, and a stack of cards with questions for the men to ask the girls. Some cards had a silly challenge instead of a question; for example, do five press-ups with your partner sitting on your back. I put in those challenges to keep everyone laughing while they were getting comfortable with asking and answering questions with each other.

The questions were wide ranging, designed to help both the men and the girls grow in feeling comfortable in talking about a breadth of topics. The questions the men asked their daughters included:

- What is one activity you wished we would do more of together, and why?
- What is something someone said to you that hurt your feelings?
- What is one thing I do that makes you feel loved and encouraged?
- What is the hardest part of your days at school?
- When do you have to be the most courageous in your week, and why?
- If you could change one thing about our family what would it be?

The daughters asked the men a similar range of questions, such as:

- What are two parts of my character (not my looks) that you really admire about me?
- What is one day you wish you could do over, and why?
- What is your favourite memory of us together?
- When you were my age, what was your favourite thing to do?
- Tell me a story of when you were most proud of me.

By enabling the men and girls to get used to asking and answering questions that built connections, many families reported a significant change in their family's dynamic. Dads began carrying the cards with them during family trips, and they even started adding more questions to their pack. Eventually, they didn't need the cards any more. I added this idea to all of our family-pairing events, including the all-age men-and-boys events and the mother–son nights. It's been a few years since I held those particular springboard resource events, but I still hear stories of how significant that new skill was for parents in helping them build their communication with their children throughout the years.

When we create springboard resources, we enable parents and extended families to leap into new areas by creating safe and comfortable opportunities for them to try to learn new skills.

## Create side-by-side experiences

One day I felt as if I was *the* terrible parent in the room. I was sitting on the floor of my child's nursery, surrounded by other pairs of tired-looking parents and three-year-olds. The leader was saying, 'We recommend you sing "Wind the Bobbin Up" with your children at home, as it will help them with their gross motor skills, as well as with their speech with consonants.' I felt a bit panicky as everyone nodded and children started shouting, 'Bobbin up!'

The problem was that I had never heard that song before. I am 90% sure it's a northern song. I was not raised up here in the wilds of the North, so I was clueless. At the time my son was significantly deaf, so his ability to accurately sing anything to me was limited, but he loved doing the signs. I knew this song would be a hit at home if I only knew it. I began to calculate how ridiculous I would look if I had to ask the lady afterwards if she would sing it to me multiple times so I could learn it. I resolved to Google it and just trust that if I watched a cartoon giraffe do the actions, that would be enough to learn it.

But then the nursery leader stood up and led the song. I was so grateful. I got to hear the song over and over, practise the actions and watch my child do it too. I got to see how much he loved it, and I learned the places where he forgot the actions. We laughed together. I watched like a hawk to learn which hand I was supposed to use and in what direction I was to point. By the time we were done, I had it figured out. I knew exactly what I was supposed to do. I knew the song, I knew how much my kid liked it and I knew I would have no problem doing it with him on my own. In five minutes that leader took me from being clueless to being confident, because she taught it to me while I was with my child, side by side.

Many times, the parents we serve can feel equally exposed when they see the vast number of recommendations we have for them. Our ideas may sound good when we talk about them, but when parents are left to try them on their own with their children, then they begin to feel overwhelmed.

We often fall into the pattern of teaching parents and children separately, but that isn't always the most effective way. We train parents in new skills in a room off to the side, and then we set them loose. Or during children's ministry, we give children spiritual tools to use, and then we send them home to explain those tools to their parents, hoping their parents will understand and know what to do with the tools.

Trying anything new spiritually with a child takes boldness, and it can be intimidating for parents. What if we could remove that effort and fear? What if we could introduce a tool to parents when they are side by side with their children? What if we could create experiences that give parents the language and skills and, most importantly, introduce them to the topic in the same space as their children? When we choose to facilitate parents' learning something alongside their children, then we create highly impactful moments with a minimal amount of time and effort.

This is more than just creating events and services that include parents with their children or teens. The trick is in creating events that proactively impart skills to them when they are side by side, which then helps both parents and children take the skill forward at the same time.

With outreach, for example, we could easily invite families to participate in one of our many outreach events, even one of those practical 'doing someone's garden' ones. These events are valuable and important in and of themselves, and they create wonderful opportunities for families to do mission together. But if we want to enable parents to coach their children through the experience, then we may need to give them some help. If we thought that some parents needed a bit of a boost, we could add, say, a pre-event bacon-butty breakfast, where we teach everyone together about the power of practical love, personal sacrifice and where God is when we serve. We could then pray together for significant things to happen during the outreach. We could even set challenges for families and individuals to try while they are at the event that reflect these teachings. Then run the event as normal.

This little bit of extra teaching would give the parents ways to talk with their children while they are on the event and give them questions to ask when they return home and debrief the experience by discussing how it felt to love people like that and what they saw God doing in their midst. By creating a side-by-side learning space, we have taken away parents' anxiety of how to explain the experience to their children and have given them what they need to coach their children in and after the ministry experience as well.

The same side-by-side technique can be applied to any situation. For example, if you want to enable parents to coach their children in worship, then create an experience where parents and children worship side by side and receive some teaching. Recently at our church, we added a five-minute launch into worship at the beginning of our service, in which I quickly taught on a different aspect of worship each week, from how to prepare our hearts, to why we sing rather than speak and what God was doing while we sang to him. These snippets of teaching equipped parents, children, teens and the rest of the congregation to enter into worship stronger, and also gave parents a language to coach their children with.

If our premise is that parents and children are on their independent journeys of faith and that their journeys impact each other, then we need to consider creating events where this happens. Side-by-side experiences are incredibly valuable for children and teens because in these experiences they can witness their parents genuinely connecting with God. One of the greatest things we can do as a church is to create these experiences for families, so they can grow in their skills of sharing their lives with God alongside each other.

## Trust yourself

Churches can create space for parents and extended families to learn and grow the skills they need to help their children and teens connect with God. Whether you pass those skills on through gathered teaching, springboard resources or side-by-side experiences, trust that God will give you ideas for how to empower parents.

Your events may look different from those in every other church in the country, and that is absolutely a good thing. There is no other church exactly like yours. Be free to innovate according to the needs of the people right in front of you. Don't limit yourself to one way of providing skills and experiences. As you slowly shift your church to being a place that encourages parents to be the primary disciplers of their children, use all the techniques you can to create an Ikea-like environment in which parents can grow. Different kinds of parents will gravitate to different types of equipping. The more we offer a spread of gathered teaching, springboard resources and side-by-side experiences, the more opportunities we create for families to engage and grow.

# 8

# Creating a multigenerational community

Recently at church one woman leaned over the shoulder of the service leader and asked if she could share something. The leader handed her the microphone and she began to talk, shaking a bit. Through tears, she thanked the congregation for being the family she didn't have. She explained that she was a single mother and relatively new to the church, and that when she first arrived she was broken and tired. But then the congregation began to invest in her little family.

The church became her brothers and sisters, calling and texting and inviting her family to join them for dinners and weekends away. People took her children on trips to the cinema, and older people volunteered to babysit and help with the shopping. Some people stepped into empty grandparent roles, and others became the chorus of encouragement. As she summarised the impact they had made on her, she was barely able to speak through her grateful tears. 'You have helped make me a better person, and most importantly, a better parent.'

God designed parenting to be rooted within the body of Christ, because it is an effective way of strengthening parents and discipling children. If we want the church to support parents and extended families, then we need to position it in a way in which people can genuinely strengthen each other. Often in today's church, we segment different populations of our communities: children, young people, young families, OAPs, those that prefer traditional services and those that don't. With this diversity has often come separation, as we homogenise groups so we can better deliver what they are looking for. While this approach has been useful in some ways, it has resulted in a lack of multigenerational community. This community is vital to creating a culture of parenting for faith.

Throughout scripture, we see multigenerational communities in action, from the Israelites worshipping together, to whole towns and villages coming together to engage with Jesus. Life itself was a process of living in multigenerational communities.

When this type of community works, everyone benefits.

For children and youth, a multigenerational community provides a place where they can always find a few individuals who are like them, who connect with God in a similar manner or who love the same things they love. They can find community with like-minded people, not just of their own age but of all ages. They can have access to older people who can look out for, advise, love and affirm them.

A multigenerational community also provides children and youth a secure place to grow into who they can be in the body of Christ. They learn how to become members of a godly community, what strengths and skills they have that are needed and appreciated by others, and how to use those skills within the community. They also learn how to love and deal with the more vulnerable people in society or the more complicated characters who are in any group. As young people grow older, they begin to take responsibility for younger members and feel the pull to be a significant presence in the lives of children.

For parents, a multigenerational community provides a peer group to learn and laugh with, where parents who are a bit ahead of them can assure them that they are normal and those who are a bit behind them can benefit from their honest and newly earned wisdom. When parents can feel the strength of having other parents and families around them, they can feel that their journey is ordinarily unique.

If the multigenerational community is functioning well, then parents also gain the wisdom and support from the generation above them. Many parents were not raised in a proactive Christian home and can feel exhausted in pioneering a new way of life for their family. When we knit our communities together, parents and carers gain access to those who have gone before them. Some are full of wisdom and helpful stories; others are full of love, compassion and understanding for what the journey is like. Parents have access to the stories of others who have already dealt with toddlers with night terrors and teens being tempted to use drugs. They can talk with those who have wisdom in how to choose a school for their kids and in what to do when their teens say they don't want to come to church.

For extended families, a multigenerational community often gives them an opportunity to stretch their wings. They can involve themselves in activities that will grow their spiritual skills with children in general, and they have access to unique opportunities to invest in the lives of the children in their families. In this community, they can be affirmed as being significant in the lives of those around them.

For the wider congregation, a multigenerational community enables all members to feel purposeful and powerful in the spiritual development of so many people around them. Older generations can feel needed and appreciated for their wisdom and love. People without children can see how truly significant they are in the lives of parents, teens and children because of who they are. When a multigenerational community works the way it is supposed to, every member feels needed, seen, loved and useful to each other's spiritual discipleship and to the kingdom of God.

If we want to create a culture of parenting for faith within our church communities, then we need to look at how we are facilitating our entire congregation to connect with each other. Connection is the oil through which spiritual influence flows, so building connection is an essential part of creating an empowering, multigenerational community.

## Tell people they are needed

It was a Sunday morning and we were two songs into an extended worship set. Out of the corner of my eye, I noticed a mother of three small children struggling to juggle the needs of her family within the confines of the pew. She was holding a songbook for her five-year-old daughter, bouncing a baby who was on the verge of crying and insisting that her two-year-old stay put even as he desperately tried to wriggle out of the pew. The mother looked exhausted and torn. Next to her in the pew was a young couple in their early 20s looking incredibly uncomfortable with the chaos near them. Behind the mother was an older couple. The older man had stopped singing and was just staring at the mass of wiggling bodies. Compassion shone all over his face. As I walked down the aisle, the man reached out and touched my arm.

'Can you please help her? She needs help,' he whispered to me.

I smiled back. 'I'm sorting something out for communion right now, but, George, you've had four children. Why don't you offer to help?'

His eyes lit up. 'Do you think I could? I'd love to walk with little Zachary.'

'Why don't you ask?'

As I continued on, I saw George lean forward, and with a smile he asked if he could help by walking around the church with the little two-year-old. The mum grinned broadly, and then George and Zachary held hands and started walking up and down the aisle together.

Seeing this, the young woman next to the family glanced over and offered to hold the songbook for the girl. The mum gratefully passed the book to the young woman, who then held it and pointed to each line of words so the child could sing along. In the space of two minutes, an exhausted mum barely holding life together was able to close her eyes and worship God while her community surrounded her and helped.

I thought a lot about that experience over the next few months. Why didn't they help her earlier? Why did they wait for so long before they offered to help? These people had known each other for years in church, and yet when it came down to it, the mum didn't ask for help and the community didn't offer. What happened here?

After church, I watched the congregation to see who talked with whom, and I saw few cross-generational conversations. Adults spoke to adults, and children spoke to children. It appeared that 'ready and available help' was not the only thing that wasn't flowing freely in the congregation: the heart of community was missing.

Throughout the years, communities have become more split. There is now an expectation that parents can cope on their own, and that those who are not related to other families are not to get involved. Those in the community can feel a silent barrier of separation. Do I know this family well enough to offer? Would they be offended or feel judged? Am I actually needed or would I just be annoying? The default of silence and separation therefore remains – families doing life on their own and capable and loving communities keeping themselves at arm's length.

One of the truths we need to speak about to our whole congregation is that everyone is needed in this community. Parents need to know it is okay to want help; they were never designed to parent on their own. The church is their extended family and friends who exist to support them and succeed as a healthy family. Congregation members need to hear the truth that they are needed: their stories are needed; their practical help is needed; their presence is needed; their affirmation and interests are necessary; and their wisdom is sought.

A question that often comes up with this topic is child protection. We fear that if we proactively encourage the community to invest in each other, then we will fling open the doors to all sorts of child-protection issues. I have worked in churches for a while, and I am acutely aware of the importance of child protection. It is important to remember, though, that we aren't saying to the congregation, 'Feel free to grab any child you want whenever you want.' Rather, we are saying, 'We are a community, not individuals isolated from one another, and we are needed in each other's lives. Talk to kids and young people. Understand that parents you know may need your input and help. Feel free to offer your friendship to families, and be gracious when the answer is no.' We can also say to parents, 'This church is full of people who can input into your children and teens. Feel free to ask people to spend time with you and your kids. And if people offer, feel free to say no. There is no judgement when people offer to help. They just want you to feel loved and to have choices. No is always okay.'

Our concern for child protection has driven a wedge of fear into our communities that needs to be put into perspective. Of course, we need to be vigilant and wise; yes, we need to have in place proper procedure. But we also need to encourage community to be community.

Some of the most significant relationships in my childhood were with older people in my church. I couldn't wait to run in to say hi to Lavina, who always gave me a mint from her handbag and asked me how my week was. Myrtle was the oldest woman I knew, but every week she would pat her hand on the seat next to her, invite me to sit down and ask me about my classes, relationships and adventures. She would also tell me surprising stories of her life and faith, and I so wanted to be like her. As I grew older, students who were coming back from university would invite me to go to lunch with them, and they would tell me all about what life was like out in the world. As a young teen, I loved going to women's events, having long conversations about menopause and marriage, and learning about how to choose a life partner through hearing stories of grief, divorce and beautifully long marriages. There was always someone to connect with, to be challenged by or to be bored with. When a child or teen isn't limited to parents or peers, then the church family becomes *their* community too.

## Create opportunities for them to hear each other

If we want children, teens and families to benefit from the wider congregation wrapping around them, then we need to help the various generations proactively connect. Achieving this is not as straightforward as it seems. Many of our communities have fallen into the habit of staying in their peer groups so that merely putting everyone in a room or event together often doesn't work. A church picnic can quickly devolve into children running around in terrifying hordes, while the teenagers huddle together on the field. Families too large to share space sit on little islands of blankets calling to each other, while those of the older generation blissfully sit in lined-up chairs watching the chaos. Even though the congregation is technically together, they are falling short of the goal.

If we want to equip a congregation to be a community, then we need to deliberately develop it. This means creating opportunities for the two most important factors for building community: hearing each other spiritually and playing together.

When we want communities to invest in each other for spiritual benefit, one of the key factors we need to facilitate is listening to each other. We are all on a journey of faith, and when we empower people of all ages to hear each other's experiences, insights and stories of life with God, we position people's hearts to want community. They become willing to learn from each other and to input into each other's lives.

An easy way to encourage listening across the generations is to provide unique opportunities for people to do so. If your church has a children's or youth ministry, often the only adults that join in are the leaders. That doesn't have to be the case. There are people in your congregation who have vast life experience, and their stories would benefit our children and young people. If the subject for the day's session is God's protection, bring in a war veteran to describe his or her experience of the situation and of God at that time. Lead a discussion enabling children and young people to share their stories of where God is in their lives, as well. Those children and teens and that soldier will be comfortable with each other from that point on. When they see each other again, they can approach each other and talk. When this reconnection happens before or after church, the adult will often be around friends, and before you know it a multigenerational conversation is going on. Many times, I have seen intergenerational friendships open up because of one invitation into a children's or youth group.

Another method to encourage listening is to create a natural communication point for people's stories. One church I know recently interviewed several children about a significant faith event and put it up on the church's Facebook page. It had a profound impact on the whole congregation, and as a result those children feel bolder in sharing their stories with others. Many churches I know use social media to facilitate the exchange of personal stories from people of all ages. It is especially meaningful when parents and their children watch those videos together at home, allowing them both to feel the same stirring of excitement and connection that comes from hearing people's stories.

Other churches encourage dinners hosted in people's homes, mixing families with singles and older people. These meals enable children, teens and adults to share life stories, hear faith journeys and be encouraged and inspired by each other. Teenagers, in particular, like these dinners as it gives them a chance to be heard and to build relationships with lots of people, increasing their independent connections with others. Congregation members love hearing stories of people's lives that are different from their own. These dinners develop a familiarity with each other that produce a greater confidence and desire to talk and connect with each other at church.

# Create opportunities for them to play together

Playing together is one of the most powerful ways to build community. When people laugh, they are less self-conscious. They connect with each other in that unique vulnerability that comes when people let their guard down and truly delight in an experience and in each other.

## The bar of fun

Often when we design an opportunity to play together across the ages, we think about creating a children's activity that adults and teens can also participate in and endure. This is often why communities shy away from creating space to play together. It can be cringeworthy and require a lot of effort. We then spend our time trying to get adults to be willing to engage and enjoy something they wouldn't naturally enjoy for the sake of the children. While many adults can do that, many others can't or won't.

But think back to your childhood. Do you remember the magical moments when your parents and their friends were playing something, and you got invited to join in? Your parents were laughing with their friends and filled with joy, and so were you. Adults playing together is irresistible to kids – they always want to join in.

I want to suggest that the easiest technique to help generations laugh together is to create genuine fun for adults that kids also can access. If an entire group of adults is having a good time, and kids and young people can participate, then it's a huge win. Teens love this approach as well, because it reinforces their growing independence and their need to belong to the group as a whole. Rather than trying to distance themselves from something 'kiddy', teens will want to participate and connect with the adults.

So, when we plan events for the whole church community, the first question we need to ask is, 'What would be genuinely fun and enjoyable for the adults?' The second needs to be, 'How do we make sure children and young people can find that accessible?'

## Let the adults loose

Many times we accidentally restrict fun, multigenerational opportunities because we haven't structured them. I am amazed at how often people in their 20s moan to me after church about how they want to see a new children's film but feel silly going alone.

'Why don't you talk to Susannah and offer to go with her kid?' I would ask, and then I'd be greeted with the blank face of someone who had never thought of that before.

Families have asked me for months why the church hasn't ever organised a camping trip for families. When I ask why they don't just post on the church's Facebook page that they are going camping and invite along anyone who wants to join, they seem genuinely surprised that that is a possibility. Our congregations sometimes need permission to just have fun with each other. We can and should encourage them to invite each other to their homes and open up their fun to others.

At a networking event a few years ago, the leader of a rural parish church told me a wonderful story of what was happening in his congregation. Several older women from the church were volunteering in the local secondary school, and they also happened to meet together regularly to knit. They decided they would invite young people from the school to join them during their weekly knitting circle in the church hall. They didn't think anyone would come, but soon eight or nine students began to attend. They'd sit together and talk about life, careers, relationships and more. What a great example for us. These older women loved knitting, and they invited others into their knitting circle. Now two generations of people are sharing life together.

## The fun of team – diversity

Another way to use fun as an intergenerational connection is to build on the power of team. Rather than build teams that make children the weak link, we can instead design games and events that reward diversity in a way that makes having children as a part of the team a strength and not a weakness.

For instance, if you are running a quiz, create questions and challenges that the teams can only achieve if they have people of all ages as part of their team. Give a warning to the teams that some of the questions and tasks require a diversity of ages and experiences. Encourage them that if they don't have a child or young person as part of their team, then they might want to try to find one who is willing to join them – and persuade their parent to loan them out. Create questions that require knowledge from all ages and experiences – political figures and cartoon characters, oldies' music and modern pop, plumbing and confectionery. Devise challenges for all sizes of people – for example, to deliver six shoes of different sizes to the front, or for one team member to pick up another and run around the room. (We recently did this at our church, and while most teams had adults running with children, one team lacked diversity, and so a man jogged while carrying his wife. Needless to say, we all cheered him on.) Feel free to make the tasks as hard as you want. For every four 'adult' questions, I would include one that a child or an over-70-year-old would be required to participate in. The split doesn't need to be 50-50; it just needs to be balanced enough so that adults of all ages are thoroughly engaged and the children can enjoy the teamwork, camaraderie and being regularly needed and useful.

The power of team naturally happens on group tasks and unites differing people into a common goal that works well across the ages.

## Be a relationship matcher

One of the strengths of being part of a church leadership is that we know a lot of our church members quite well; we have become specialists of our communities. If our goal is to create a multigenerational community to surround parents and extended families, then sometimes we need to connect people to each other, enabling, for example, isolated families to meet those who can help.

Recently a couple was in hospital, as the wife was giving birth. Soon after the healthy delivery of their boy, the doctors told the parents that their child had Down's syndrome. The parents were not sure how to respond. When their church heard the news, the leader called an older family in the congregation who also had a child with Down's syndrome and asked them to come alongside this new family. With the new parents' permission, they showed up at the hospital with balloons and joyful faces to congratulate the parents on the birth of a child they knew would be a blessing to them all. They answered their questions, created space for their emotions and encouraged them that they would walk the journey with them. For these new parents trying to face an uncertain future, that relationship became a lifeline of encouragement.

In one church I was at, we noticed some families struggling with children they had to manage, so we offered a 'buddy' for the first part of the service. Many of our youth volunteered to support these families, and every Sunday these 'buddies' would greet and sit with the larger families who needed help. Another church created an exciting innovation for children's dedications and baptisms when the parents were new Christians and lacking Christian extended family. For those parents who wanted it, the church invited individuals and families to enter into the role of family encouragers, focusing on encouraging and supporting the parents in figuring out how to spiritually parent their children. These people were committed to praying for the new parents, helping them and being ready to answer the phone and chat whenever the parents had a question about how to spiritually support their children.

So many families could benefit from what people in our congregation can give, and so many of our church members would benefit from being needed by a family. We can be the matchmakers that facilitate the right introductions among people.

## Use existing structures to create opportunities for people to be the body of Christ

When people serve alongside each other, they appreciate each other; they disciple each other. When people join a church, we encourage them to get involved on a serving team, partially because it helps them feel connected as well as needed. When people are needed and serving together, they get to know each other and bless each other. Too often, though, our children and teens are excluded from that experience.

Allowing children and teens to serve on teams is one of the most powerful methods for building intergenerational relationships that have spiritual impact. As a youth pastor, whenever my teens joined a team, I saw their engagement with God dramatically rise.

This is one of the areas of growth that home and family cannot provide. Home cannot provide teens with the opportunity to be exposed to a wide range of non-related individuals who gather around a mission or task. Home cannot give teens a common place to discover what they as individuals can bring to the rest of the church. Home can help children and teens discover their passions and skills, and can disciple them in the beginning to use those skills, but it is within the team of the wider body of Christ that children and teens can refine who they are as part of the whole. This is the part that the church is designed to be in the life of children and teens. We wrap ourselves around parents and extended family to be their supporters and encouragers, and we also become a secure place for their children to flourish and discover their part in the wider Christian community.[6]

My son loves helping with the sound equipment at church. He isn't old enough to bear any responsibility yet, but the men and women on the sound and worship teams welcome him wholeheartedly. I regularly see him with headphones on just listening as the sound guy adjusts levels during worship. After church, I see members of the band curled on the floor next to him teaching him which cable goes into which plug, and how to coil the cables correctly. He glows when he is helping those teams, and as a parent I am so grateful. My church is giving my son what I cannot: an invitation to be purposeful and to team up with people who aren't his natural family.

## Tweak timings

Often it is hard to build a multigenerational church because the generations rarely blend. We plan evening events that take place after young children's bedtimes, and we schedule services with lots of space between them in order to facilitate the flow of people. Too often it just seems to take a lot of effort to schedule multigenerational opportunities. But there are ways we can create opportunities for connections by slightly tweaking the timings of what we do. What if, instead of doing team meetings in the evenings, we changed them to breakfast meetings or to tea on a Sunday? What if we encouraged home groups to start half an hour earlier to allow some members to interact with the children in the home and eat pudding together with them? What if we began to look at our structures to ensure that we aren't isolating the generations by our scheduling? Sometimes it is in small changes that the biggest opportunities are waiting to be discovered.

## Create it unique to you

Every community is different, and how your church family finds places to hear each other spiritually and have fun together will look quite unique in every way. Enjoy the pioneering journey of helping people find the joy of being a loving, supportive community for each other.

# 9

# Encouraging parenting for faith in services

Our main services are one of the central places for the culture of our church to be expressed and reinforced, so they are a crucial opportunity to empower and support parenting for faith as a part of that culture.

There are two main considerations for how to do this well:

1  how we utilise the up-front presentation and structure of an average service to affirm and reinforce the messages of parenting for faith for the whole congregation;
2  if children are present, how we proactively facilitate parents in the midst of the service.

## Up-front presentation

What we talk about from the front of church matters. It is our most public articulation of what is important to us as a group of people. We have limited time during a service, so we try to ensure that what we say, give time to and create space for is finely tuned to achieve what we feel is important for our services to deliver. Communicating a vision for parenting for faith can often get squished out of that priority list. It is often only referenced as a preface to the latest notice about the upcoming course or parents' night. But if we want to create a self-sustaining, organic culture of parenting for faith within our congregations, we need to integrate the values of it into our core set of what we do from the front. That doesn't mean, however, that it requires more dedicated time. My suggestion is not that we give more chunks of teaching or notices to parenting for faith, but rather own it as a key value that gets shared as part of the standard service.

As part of any service, we as leaders seem to be constantly holding up vision, whether a vision of life with Jesus, of a new discipleship initiative or of how tasty the next all-church breakfast is going to be. Congregations expect to be envisioned at church.

The first step to enabling individuals to go on a parenting-for-faith journey is to give them vision. We have already discussed creating an Ikea-like vision for families, speaking foundational truths to them and facilitating a community of storytellers. These three skills are crucial for the creation of a vision, led from the front, of parenting for faith as part of daily life. What sharing vision doesn't require, though, is regular slots of people standing up droning on and on about parenting for faith being important. Rather, I want to suggest that we gently weave these skills into what we do on a Sunday.

## Create an Ikea-like vision

For example, approaching families with an Ikea-like selection of unique choices can be easily woven into sermons. What if we asked that every person who preached included just one window into their own parenting-for-faith journey, or suggest in one sentence how the topic could be applied either to parenting or the spiritual life of a child or teen? It could be very small; during a sermon about God's complete forgiveness the speaker could drop in an illustration, such as: 'I was talking to my son about this the other day during our night highlights. We usually at night just lie on the floor and ask each other our top three headlines of the day. As I was telling him my most frustrating part of my day, it suddenly hit me that I hadn't forgiven that man. It was churning in me.' Or while applying the story of the talents, people can be momentarily encouraged with something like the following:

This applies to all disciples of God. Our teens and children are just as accountable as we are to God for the gifts he has given them and how they are using those gifts for the kingdom. If you have young people who know God in your life, whether you are a parent, grandparent, godparent, aunt, uncle or even a family friend, I ask you, 'How are you encouraging them and affirming their gifts? How are you inviting them to use those gifts in your home and our church?' You will know how to do this best, but if you aren't sure, you might want to start by just praying and noticing what God has gifted them with, and telling them how much you appreciate that gift, and then see what is next.

Creating an Ikea culture isn't always about listing things for parents to do. It's about surrounding them with stories and challenges that provide an environment where they become accustomed to hearing, over and over, a wide variety of moments and opportunities to encourage their children's connection with God.

## Be the truth-teller

Part of leading a service is about creating a language of familiarity and truth. We can drip-feed some of the key truths we want parents, extended families and congregations to understand into the usual pattern of our Sunday patter:

We are all on our journeys of faith, side by side, adults, children, Ghanaians and British. We welcome you to join us for this part of your journey!

Or if there is a moment in your service when the children leave to go to their groups, you can drop in:

We as a church love when we get to be a small part of the wonderful stuff you are already doing with your children all week. This is the time when we as a community have the privilege of learning and worshipping together in peer groups, so if your children would like to go into their age groups, then follow Sally…

We as leaders can periodically drop most of the key truths we discussed in Chapter 2 into the regular service conversation.

An important reason for doing this is that the ordinary language of the service is foundational to church culture – we not only set down the culture for parents and carers, but also for how the entire congregation views parenting, children and teens, and the place of the church within it. Young adults, teens and even children may hear these words as well. In how we create a culture from the front of church, we are discipling the next generation of parents.

## Community storytelling

Most churches I know don't regularly have storytelling or testimony slots as part of their Sunday service but, if you do, consider enabling families to tell their stories as part of the regular rotation. Often we herald the big life-transforming adult stories, of drugs or loss, and forget that the small family moments, say, of battling night-terrors, can be just as significant. Congregations need to hear both.

When interviewing a parent who is walking through chronic pain, it can make such a statement to the congregation to ask the question, 'How have you been spiritually walking this with your children?' If you have people sharing how they learned to love the Bible, don't forget to include children and young people who can tell stories of how their gran or parents first opened them to the love of it. If your church structure already includes stories, just add that subtle strand to what you are already doing.

Our presentations at the front during a service signal the kind of culture we are curating. It only takes a little tweak to add the values of parenting for faith to it.

# Facilitating parents

If your church has parents and children in a service together for any length of time, then you have a fantastic opportunity to encourage and equip parents within a service.

We have already discussed many ideas for how to facilitate parents to learn and use skills within the service. From enabling multigenerational community to creating springboard resources, there is a lot we can do to help parents from the sides. But what about up front? What can we do as part of the structure of the service that will make it easier for parents through a service?

## The Hint Drop

Many times during a service, we want to create space for parents to help their children engage with what is going on, but how we do this communicates our care and value significantly for parents.

One of parents' biggest stresses is feeling exposed. As I type this, I am sitting in a restaurant half a metre away from a screaming two-year-old. His parents are handling the situation beautifully, but I can sense their intense internal pressure to deal with it quickly. They are glancing around to gauge the response of those in the restaurant and are very exposed. They feel like we are all watching how they will handle the challenge.

When we are in a service, parents can feel similarly exposed. So, by adding an instruction from the front, such as 'Parents, please bring your children down to the front' or 'Parents, please open your booklets and show them to your children', we can make parents feel like they are in the spotlight. Their leader has asked them to do something, and they now either have to comply and put their parenting skills on show or have to admit to the whole congregation that they can't make it happen. It adds an incredible pressure to parents, which they don't thank us for.

One of our key values should be for parents to feel that they are in charge of their children's spiritual engagement and that their best is enough. To communicate this well, while also creating opportunities for parents to coach their children, try the Hint Drop.

The Hint Drop suggests without the expectation of obedience. It invites people into an Ikea moment, while knowing that some people won't want to accept the invitation. Instead of saying 'Parents, please bring your children down to the front', we could say, 'For everyone, including families, feel free to be wherever works best for you. We've created space at the front if that is helpful for you, but feel free to settle wherever you like.' Instead of saying 'Parents, please open your booklets and show them to your children', try 'If reading and following along is something that you and your family like to do, booklets are available for you to use as you like. Adults, if you don't have children but would benefit from a visual aid, feel free to grab one as well.'

From 'Some people like to cuddle their kid while praying, but whatever you do, get comfy as we confess to God' to 'We are going to do the service a bit differently today as it is Remembrance Day, so if you are with someone who may benefit from some coaching through the service, you might want to take an opportunity through the worship to whisper to them about what this day is. We will be talking about it a bit more after worship', the Hint Drop gives parents a clue of what we have available to them and nudges them to use skills they already have while also communicating that there is no pressure on them to engage in a particular way.

Congregations have all types of families and people. Some families have complicated lives, so we shouldn't always assume that there are two married Christian parents present and available in a service. Remembering to use phrases such as 'parents and carers', being aware that some children or parents may have additional needs or disabilities, and factoring in the logistics of our suggestions means that we won't be setting families up for failure. As we create hints to drop, allow for families of all shapes and abilities to engage. It's part of the Ikea range.

The Hint Drop is a good balance between leaving parents completely on their own and being too directive.

## Accessible language

One of the skills we give parents is the ability to help their children make sense of the world and, in particular, the spiritual aspects of life. We want parents to become proficient at explaining where God is and engaging with what he is doing, including in church services. But we can be a significant blessing if we don't make parents work too hard. Children and teens need to feel they can understand and participate in church if they are going to want to continue in it. While their parents or carers will need to explain some bits, the more we can make our language accessible to children and teens, the more they will be able to engage on their own. Parents are also listening, and how we explain things will soon become the language that parents reinforce.

Leaders often think 'accessible language' means 'dumbing it down', but it is about removing as many hindrances as possible. Rather than thinking about what a child needs to hear, I find it helpful to focus on language that will enable a 40-year-old who is new to church to engage with the service. I'm not talking about changing the *content* of the service, but the *language*. If your church does readings from the Bible, try adding a few sentences that say, 'We believe God gave us his words to strengthen, encourage and challenge us, to know him better, and to know how to walk with him. Let's get ready to hear what God will say to us as we listen to his words now.'

In general, to make language accessible consider:

- Taking out shorthand Christian terms – we overuse some words, such as 'bless', 'provision' and 'presence', because they are easy for us to use. But they are vague to listeners who don't know the Christian language. Try to use other words to say the same thing.

- Explain three things – often we can just explain how to engage with whatever activity is next: 'Please stand'. Instead, explain three things: what you as a leader are going to do, what they as a congregation are going to do and, most importantly, what God is going to do.

## Easy does it

While there have been many suggestions in this chapter of how to shape our up-front presentation to create a culture of parenting for faith, as well as the language we can use to facilitate parents within the room, don't feel the pressure to implement everything straightaway. Every little helps when it comes to this, and parents will be profoundly grateful for every change you make to shape a culture where they can flourish.

# 10

# Parenting for faith
# and children's ministry

If we believe in equipping parents to help their children connect with God in everyday life, then that belief will influence how we approach everything in our youth and children's ministry. The discipleship impact we have will grow exponentially as we make the support structure surrounding children and youth as robust and capable as possible. If we want to see children and young people flourishing, then we need to see parents and extended families as parts of the discipleship equation.

A common analogy leaders use to describe how youth or children's ministries work with parents is that of a rowboat with two oars. The rowboat symbolises the discipleship of a child or young person with one oar designed for parents and the other for the church's ministry. If a parent is in the boat alone and trying to row with one oar, the boat will go in circles. Likewise, if the children's ministry is alone and trying to row with only one oar, the boat will go in circles. The illustration highlights that if we 'partner' with parents, rowing side by side, then together we will move children's and young people's discipleship forward.

On the face of it, that analogy makes sense. We like the image. It feels nice. It is a view of partnership and togetherness, with us working hard on our oar and parents working hard on theirs, 50-50, side by side.

Except that it's wrong. And it can create significant problems.

I love to take my son rowing. We live near a lovely river and in a beautiful, calm place where we can rent a rowboat and row ourselves around a few bends. When my son was young, I used to take him rowing often. He would talk non-stop, point at nature, scream at random movements in the water and laugh. I would row us around, admire the natural beauty and love the physical challenge.

Then he got old enough to want to row with me – me on one oar and him on the other – and it got complicated. Suddenly my idyllic experience became an exercise in communication and teamwork. It was exhausting. We had to coordinate our oars and constantly talk about which direction to row and how to do it. I had to instruct him how to lift his oar out of the water so that I could paddle harder to make a turn. Sometimes he would get distracted and accidentally drag his oar in the water, slowing us down, or he would purposely row against me to take us in a different direction. Occasionally I would slack off, and he would be frustrated with me because he was trying hard to row well. We ended up having to take turns rowing as we both found it too frustrating to do it together. When we both felt responsible for our own half of a 'together' job, it required too much from both of us.

Partnership is hard because it requires shared responsibility and shared authority. We see this partnership at work in marriage, which is about the dance of shared responsibility, and also in formal work environments, which demand the same balance. Partnership is a weighty word and a powerful concept.

But we aren't partners with parents. The church is the supporting community around parents and extended family; we aren't side-by-side equal partners. Parents don't have to defer to us, prioritise our input or consult with us before they make decisions. We aren't that powerful, nor do we have that much authority in the lives of children.

We aren't partners rowing in a boat side by side. The more that we *think* we are, the more difficult our relationships with parents are going to be. We will both feel that tension of differing opinions, the stress of trying to pull in the same direction, and the pressure to communicate in a way that will make the awkward partnership work.

When we embrace that we aren't co-partners with parents, we as children's leaders can be free to purely focus on doing our parts well. We can teach children valuable concepts and give them new experiences and opportunities that families on their own can't give. For example, we can add fantastic peer-specific teaching, allowing children to wrestle with ideas, encounter God and discuss life with God with people their own age. In addition, children's ministries can significantly shape children's understanding of God.

We can be parents' support community, equipping and honouring them and reinforcing what they are doing. We can position our ministries to be another strand of the equipping and encouragement that they are receiving.

We can be empowering community for children, loving them and enabling them to step into their part of the body of Christ. Being community for children includes helping them to become involved in leading and to participate in the church's teams and outreach events, as well as in their own groups. It means supporting the wider congregation to get involved in children's lives and to enable the multigenerational aspect of the church.

If we can get our heads around this, then by making a few adjustments we can become an incredibly empowering force for children's parents, carers and extended families.

Children's leaders do some fantastic ministry. We know how to share stories creatively, design crafts that are unique and comfortably talk about God with children. We can empower children to meet with God and we can explain complex theology in a simple, accessible way. Parents sincerely appreciate our contribution to their children's spiritual growth. They are relieved and grateful to have us in their children's lives, and we love helping their children to connect with God and grow with him. But what can we do within our children's ministry realms to encourage and equip parents to do their role well?

# Communication

## Listen to parents

Often we plan our curriculum and strategy for the term or year ahead without considering parents. Some of us just continue rolling out the next set of curriculum we receive from the curriculum plan. Others of us look at what we've done over the past year, think about where the children are spiritually, look at some curriculums we like, and then decide what we want to do next.

But what would happen if one of the factors we used to choose curriculum was the needs of the parents?

One of our many strengths as children's leaders is in strategically covering topics. We can absolutely nail a series on the fruit of the Spirit or the parables of Jesus. What if we went to parents and said, 'You are on the front lines of your children's spiritual journeys. In what areas do you feel they need a significant leap forward? What topic would serve you well if we covered it? How is it going with your children? What series could we wade into that would bless you and your children and help add momentum to what you are doing?'

I've known many churches that build in a parent-connection moment before they plan for the next term. Some build it into a parents' meeting, whether it be during a breakfast before church or in an evening. Other churches gather parents' input by online polling or asking for feedback through email.

Inviting parents into the conversation doesn't mean their input is the only consideration in curriculum planning. Often it may mean dropping in only one or two weeks of specific teaching in response to what parents have shared. But it is significant for parents to realise that we are trusting them to know what is happening in their children's lives and to know that they can ask us to help their children take the next steps.

For the topics that you don't choose to cover in the children's ministry, feel free to go back to the parents with some next steps they can take personally. For example:

> You mentioned that it might be helpful for us to do a session on the practicalities of Jesus' resurrection. It is a good topic to cover, but unfortunately, I don't think we can fit that into the curriculum this term. But I don't want to leave you hanging so I found some resources that may help. This short book might help you think through the arguments and theology behind the resurrection; it very much helped me. If you prefer to watch something, I found this clip to be fantastic, as I'm sometimes too tired to read. If you wanted something for him to engage with directly because he's asking for something like that, then this book is written specifically for kids, or he could watch that particular Alpha video here! I've also put that topic on the list to think about for next term.

When we include parents' views into our planning, we not only serve parents well but also their ideas are valuable for assessing what would be most helpful for the children we serve.

## Facilitate their conversations

It is a classic conundrum. After you have done much planning and preparation and have led a fairly successful morning, little Ahmed leaves your group to be greeted by his parents. You hear through the cacophony, 'So what did you do in the group today?' You see the kid's shoulders shrug, and then he says, 'I don't know. I made a slingshot!' His mum pats him on the head and smiles. 'Ooh, that's nice,' she replies. You want to call out, 'We did more than that! We shared about fear, and prayed, and...'

It can often feel like there is a disconnect between what we do in the group and what gets communicated to parents. When we primarily focus on the quality of the children's ministry we're doing, then parents not hearing about it can be sad but ultimately unimportant. But if we focus on making our children's ministry another key strand in the encouragement and equipping that we offer to parents, then this disconnect becomes a significant hurdle we need to conquer.

Many of us have tried to solve this problem by sharing with parents what we cover in each session through email, signs at the door or sending letters home. Some of us have even tried to create follow-up activities for parents to do with their children at home. We try to give parents something to do to follow up on what we just did in the session. I have talked with many churches who feel that if they make the Sunday-morning kids' ministry the big spiritual splash of the week, then families can just focus on keeping the topic going for the rest of the week. This unintentionally centres the discipleship back within the church, making what happened at church to be the main thrust of discipleship parents then need to continue, rather than the other way around.

So, how can we communicate to parents in a way that keeps the centre of discipleship firmly with them, while still using Sunday morning as a significant tool for parents to engage with?

I find it is most helpful to facilitate parents' conversations with children and to create opportunities for them to use the core skills we have been giving them. Instead of saying, 'We covered David and Goliath and how God makes us brave,' try giving parents some introductions into how to use the skills we have been giving them.

For example:

1  When sharing with parents what you covered during the session, tell them not only what you taught, but also what you asked the children to think about and to share and how they engaged with God. So, instead of, 'We covered how God makes us brave through acting out the story of David and Goliath with props', try sharing, 'We talked about where God is when we are afraid and what he does in response. After reading the story of David and Goliath, we shared stories of where in our lives we are afraid, and then we asked God what he was going to do in response. We then spent some time drawing where God is in that fear.' As you can see, the first communication only allows parents to ask their children about the activity in the group, but the second communication invites parents to ask their children about what they shared and opens up a discussion about fear and connection with God.

2  It is better to give parents skills to use rather than activities to do. Rather than suggest, 'Make a plan for conquering something scary this week', try to suggest openings for parents to explore: 'Giving your children an insight into how you walk through scary times with God is valuable for them. If you feel it is right, create a window into your life around this subject. You could share a story about something that happened in your past when you were facing a situation that seemed hopeless and you were afraid, and then share how you and God made that journey together. Your story could be about friends, a work situation or anything else, and it can form the idea of how the story of David and Goliath is real and meaningful for their lives with God today. You could even create a window into your present life and share with your child how you are currently facing something that seems like a big Goliath. You could share how you are feeling about it and what you are doing to see and obey God in it.'

# Giving them the skills before they need them

I recently joined a gym. One of the first things they do after processing your payment is to recommend that you book an induction session before your first visit to orient you to the gym. But I had belonged to a gym before – albeit 15 years prior – and so I thought, 'How much can gyms have changed? I don't want to have to follow a person around for an hour being lectured to on how to pick up and put down a weight. No thank you. I'll skip it.'

On my first day, I smugly walked into the building in my shiny new workout gear and instantly hit a wall of my own ignorance. I couldn't find the changing rooms or the toilet. I went upstairs and downstairs. I looked in the spin-class studio. Nowhere. I couldn't figure out how to open the lockers in the main room. I had to flag down a huge bodybuilder, who showed me that I was turning the handle the wrong way. I threw my stuff in, discovered my lock didn't fit and everything else continued downhill from there. From being thrown off the stair stepper, because I didn't push the right button, to being told off by a group of teenagers for not locking my weights back correctly, I had a mess of a first day. It was deeply embarrassing. I booked an induction.

With just one half-hour tour, the gym world was no longer a mystery. After my induction, I breezed into the women's changing room, used my newly purchased proper lock and knew the sequence of programming intervals on the elliptical machine. I used resistance machines like a champ, smoothly navigated the free-weights room and knew how to wait subtly in a queue for a rowing machine. I was like a professional. If only I had gotten the skills before I needed them.

Parents often feel like uninitiated novices when they engage with our children's ministry. We do wonderful, spiritual activities with their children, and then we send the children home to parents who are not prepared and don't know how to engage with what we are doing.

But it doesn't need to be that way. We can make sure the parents we work with never feel out of their depth or unprepared. We can do this by making sure they have the skills they need ahead of time.

Have a look at the curriculum you are covering in the next few terms. What are the topics, and what skills do parents need to have to be able to flourish in those topics?

Before we start covering a topic with children, we need to think through how to give parents the confidence to help their children respond to what they will be learning. For instance, if we are talking about mission and sharing faith, parents need time to think about how to answer questions about people of different faiths and ways to talk about family members who aren't Christians.

Communicating with parents can happen in many different ways, such as making available to them books and videos for the few months before we start covering a topic or putting on a parents' night to explain what we will be covering and to give parents the skills they need to empower their child well.

As the programme is running, ensure that if a child is given a spiritual tool – for example, how to read the Bible or how to pray for friends – the parent has access to it as well. Parents run into this frustration all the time: the school teaches children maths in a certain way, and then parents are expected to help them with their homework, even though they don't know all the new vocabulary and techniques their children have just learned. In order for parents to access the tools they need in an Ikea-like way, some people show videos, organise breakfasts or even create multigenerational experiences within the kid's ministry.

## Facilitate their involvement in significant key moments

When we are passionate about discipling children, we can create significant opportunities within our groups for them to connect with God. Early in my career after one particular service, I was talking to a dad about what we did in the morning session, and his daughter jumped in and shared how she spoke to God about her fear of sharks and she felt peaceful now and wasn't scared any more. As she bounced away, the dad turned to me and said, 'We've been praying and talking about this with her for ages. I'm so happy for her. I just wish I could have been there to be a part of it.'

I felt sick. This parent didn't know that fear was the topic for the day, and I had stolen from him the opportunity to be a part of helping his child conquer this particular fear. There are so many significant spiritual things we do in children's ministry without considering that parents might want to be a part of them. Let's not steal these moments from parents. Instead, let's invite them to decide what *they* want to do. It doesn't take a huge amount of effort or adjustment, but just that little shift in how we communicate can be empowering for them.

You could try something like this:

> Hey, parents, we are talking about persecution next week in children's groups. If you wanted to be the one to introduce your kids to this topic, we have found a website that could be helpful for you. We recognise that this might be a tough subject for some, and if you would rather not have your children in the session, we understand. We won't be showing any videos or using any graphic details, but you know your child best.

Over the years, I have had a few parents keep their children out of specific sessions for a variety of reasons: sometimes because they wanted to be the person to introduce that idea and they felt their children weren't ready yet, and other times because they felt their child couldn't handle the topic. I know other parents who took the opportunity to have that conversation first, so on the Sunday their children were proactively telling their recent stories and new information. Still others chose to come into the session and join in the group so they would have the same information their children were getting. In one instance, a child had recently suffered the loss of his grandad, and his mum chose to join her child in our session on Jesus raising people from the dead, in order to reinforce their own discussions of life after death.

When we empower parents to be the main ones to have significant conversations with their children, then they can feel more in control of how to engage.

## Turn kids towards their parents

It's not just parents who fall into the trap of thinking the church is the only place to learn things about God. Children can also come to think that the church is where they receive their main spiritual input. One of the unique aspects of our position is that we can teach children to see their parents as spiritually wise people to partner with as they journey with God. The more we can encourage and bless the parent–child relationship, the better for all involved.

One way to do this is to switch the emphasis of any take-home suggestions. Instead of sending home suggested activities that place the focus on *parents* needing to do something with their children, I tend to send home activities and projects that motivate *children* to draw on parents' skills. For example: 'Ask an adult, "What is the most surprising time in your life when God did something?" Write down the answer. Then write down your answer to the same question.' Or: 'Watch an adult and draw a picture of when that adult connects with God. Remember that it may not look like anything special. You may have to ask the person to let you know when he or she feels most close to God. Then draw a picture of when you feel most connected to God in your week.' In doing this, we are motivating children to learn something from their parents.

## Keep going

Church-based ministry to children is an important strand of children's discipleship. We are able to give children experiences of God and of being part of God's community that they can't get at home. Keep going! But as we continue to put on great programmes for children, let's up our game in communicating with parents and in equipping them with the skills they need, so we can see the children we love and serve flourish in being discipled every day of their lives.

# 11

# Parenting for faith and youth ministry

When one thinks of youth ministry, the phrase 'equipping parents' isn't usually among the top ten things that come to mind. Leading youth ministry has historically involved endless rounds of deep conversations, wild games, silly dress-up and late-night chats. It requires the planning of missions trips and helping young people learn to navigate tough life choices. It means designing a programme of relationships to enable young people to grow in their independence and discover who they are and who God is in a safe, loving and fun Christian environment.

But leading youth ministry is also an excellent opportunity to be the prime encouragers to parents through this time of their children's growth and experimentation.

When I first got involved in youth ministry, I only thought about parents as logistical hoops to jump through. But they sure made themselves known. Some were so relaxed, I could never get them to respond; others would feedback about everything. Some were desperate to push me to get more involved with their children, provide better groups, and take them and their friends out to coffee. It seemed I could never do enough for them. Others seemed uninterested to the point that I would be concerned. I think most of us who got involved in youth ministry never bargained for the amount of parent ministry we ended up doing.

But that is why we are already perfectly positioned to equip and empower parents of teenagers. We are already in a relationship with both parents and their teens. We are already in the midst of their families and lives. Rather than just aim to get parents to focus on young people, we can turn this involvement into one of the biggest strengths of our ministries.

Young people need their parents. They need their parents' love and wisdom; they need their parents to set boundaries for them and coach them. Young people need to be parented, but often parents lose confidence just when their teenagers need them the most. We can be a vital voice that helps parents as their teens journey with God.

The beginning of this book details how we as individuals can envision and equip parents. We talked about being Ikea rather than a dentist, offering visionary options and opportunities for parents to find their own path of parenting for faith. We discussed speaking the truth to parents, reaffirming their position and power in their children's lives and what that looks like in reality. We talked about building a community of stories around them to make them feel normal and find inspiration and encouragement from the journey of others. We then talked about coaching parents together as well as individually and being willing to function as a help desk to answer their questions.

If you as a leader did all those things, the parents you serve would flourish. Even if you did nothing else, the impact you would make on the young people and the environment that they live in would be massively significant.

In this chapter, I'm going to highlight some additional things that we as youth ministry can do to equip and support parents, but please do not underestimate the power of just one person fully embracing the skills of envisioning and equipping. If you skipped the previous chapter, on children's ministry, I encourage you to read that, as some of the principles outlined there also apply to youth ministry.

What are some fundamental principles that we as youth leaders can have to help parents?

# Invest in relationships with parents

Parents who think that they need to chase us all the time can feel incredibly frustrated and devalued. If we want to affirm and support parents, then we need to be proactive in getting to know them. Our primary focus can still be on the youth, but if parents know that we are available and open to them, and are *for* them and their relationship with their children, then a platform of support and honesty can be established.

# Help young people build and maintain a connection with their parents

Research has shown how important young people's relationship with their parents is for the development of their faith. When we deliberately choose to be pro-parent, therefore, we can facilitate one of the biggest gifts there is for a young person's faith.

## Talk about parents behind their back

Young people love moaning about their parents. It's one of the ways they set out their independence and begin to process that their parents aren't perfect. But young people are also secretly proud of their parents and love them very much. We can be the people who also bring to the table praise and admiration for their parents. 'I love how gentle your dad is; I so want to be like him when I'm a dad' can make a teen boy smile. 'Your mum is a remarkable leader. I love watching her lead the worship team; I learn so much.' As they go on their process of individuation, it is important that we help that to be a positive experience. We don't need to argue with them or disagree with their assessment of their parents, but we can listen without affirming the negative. It's just as easy to say, 'Sounds like you had a frustrating day' rather than, 'Ugh, parents are the worst. I hated when my parents did that too.' Then, when the topic is no longer current, drop in some positive comments.

We can also be the observers of relationship. For example: 'I'm not sure you know how much your dad is proud of you. He went on and on about how you revised for your exams. Your perseverance really made him proud.' Or: 'Look how happy your mum is. She just lights up when you come to church with her.'

## Encourage the parent as a wise option

As teens ponder decisions about life, often we can become a critical part of the process. Once in a while, it is helpful to encourage the young people to talk to their parents. For example: 'That is tricky. What advice did your dad have?' Or: 'On questions like that, I'd usually ask my mum, as I remember she went through something similar around my age. Do you think your mum could help shed some light on the subject?' When we encourage young people to talk to their parents and to see them as wise and loving people who can help, we aren't cutting them off from our help but reaffirming the presence and availability of wise people in their lives.

## Create experiences for them to play and work together

Sometimes young people need a bit of nudging to remember how much fun they can have with their parents. As a ministry, we can create events for parents and young people to experience that again. Take them away on a camping trip, or have a competition night. Put them in pairs and run a table-tennis tournament or a Lego-building contest. Organise a ministry trip for a group of adults and teens together. Find something that adults and teens would love to do and make it happen. From paintballing to escape rooms to simple water-balloon fights, enable parents and teens to laugh and play together. The fun builds connection. You can also build into those events space for profound questions, revelations and talking about real and current issues in the lives of the parents, where they can begin to model authentic conversation and sharing about God in their lives today.

## Praise children to their parents

This suggestion sounds simple, but many parents rarely hear praise about their teens. Statements such as, 'He shows such compassion sometimes, it is quite moving. You did a good job with him', make parents' hearts explode with pride. We often get to see beautiful parts of their teens' characters, and it encourages parents to hear that we are seeing the fruit of who God made their children to be and how well they have parented them so far. I tend to go with general character traits, as I don't want to make the young people feel like I will violate their privacy to their parents, but I don't mind talking about anything a young person has done for me.

# Communicate well

For parents, the more information they have, the better. It makes them feel safe, and it gives them a basis for conversations with their children. Even simple things, such as what topics you are discussing on what day, can be of huge benefit to parents.

One youth ministry did a series on 'God in the everyday' and invited members of the congregation to tell stories of their lives and where they see God, whether while doing their accountancy job or during a social-work visit. The youth worker sent to parents a schedule of the series, including who was speaking and what their job was. The parents looked forward to asking their young people all about the speaker and what they said. Parents reported it made for a vibrant conversation over lunch, and they enjoyed discussing the insights their young people had.

It is important to communicate not just what topics you are covering, but how you are going to be covering them, especially if a topic is controversial. You can guarantee some panicky phone calls when you put up on a term card 'Homosexuality – 22 May'. If the topics are in any way controversial, create a method of communication that loops parents into the topic. You could email your outline for the talk two weeks ahead of time, or publish a parents-only summary of the term with a few paragraphs that highlight your main approaches and conclusions for the subjects you will be covering. Some youth ministries run open nights where the youth workers sit with parents and discuss the topic and enable the parents to talk with each other about how they feel and how they approach that issue with their children.

When we communicate well, parents can feel empowered to decide how they want to utilise what we are doing in how they are parenting.

## Be the mine finder

Another thing we can do to empower parents is to help them understand the landscape that their teens are living in. Teens are in the stage of separating themselves from their parents, making choices and mistakes, and learning to decide what information about themselves they want to share and what they don't. Most parents will have become accustomed to their children being their prime source of information about what stresses their children are under. As the children get older, some information can begin to drop out and parents can become out of touch with situations in the world that are prevalent in youth culture. If parents don't know what to look out for, then they are out of pace with where they need to be to parent for faith well.

As youth leaders, we are required to live in and understand the world of young people. We can be window-openers for parents, enabling them to become aware of what is happening in youth culture today. I know one youth worker who each term would send out a youth culture update, which would share the latest apps to watch out for, television programmes that were controversial, updates in school requirements, examples of cyber bullying and the most recent research about youth culture. Parents loved it and felt better able to have conversations, because they knew what their children were dealing with.

## Help them adapt their skills

As youth leaders, we can help parents learn how to grow and adapt for the season their children are in and learn the skills they still need for this part of their children's lives. Parents need skills in how to connect with their children, how to position themselves to influence their children, how to disciple them proactively and how to help them connect with God. The skills that they crave usually revolve around discipline and freedom, helping their teens navigate the world as a Christian and how much to get involved spiritually with their child.

If you want to have a look at some of the core skills and how we help parents adapt them, check out **parentingforfaith.org**. You may want to run a Parenting for Faith course just for the parents of teens, training them how to apply the core skills to their season as they learn them.

## Keep going

Youth leaders, of course, are primarily called to young people, and it is important to stay focused on them. Young people need us to help them flex their spiritual muscles and learn what it is to be a part of the wider body of Christ. As we help them to explore their faith and integrate into the community of believers, we can with little extra effort also empower their parents to use the thousands of hours a year they have with their teenager to continue to disciple them in their connection with God.

# 12

# Parenting for faith on the fringes

When I first started to equip people to parent for faith, I was on a high. Children and young people were growing in faith, and parents and grandparents were encouraged and excited about what they were doing. As I began to play with my understanding of children and young people's discipleship, and the role of the church within it, something niggled at the back of my mind. I'm sure it's occasionally been in the back of yours too.

Equipping active Christian parents makes sense. We can completely picture how it could work. But what about the children and young people who don't have Christian parents? What about our fringe families who float into the church a few times a year, who we would think of as marginal Christians? What about families who attend our churches to get their children into primary or secondary school, or the community ones who we have never seen until they want to get married, baptise or dedicate their children, or have us perform a funeral service? What about the parents who attend our dads-and-tots mornings, or just come to our large Christmas events? What about the parents of the children we see during our school visits?

What is the 'biblical plan' for the children of the unchurched? If parents are not Christians or aren't spiritually active, should the church step in and take on the spiritual parenting role?

My short answer is: parents are parents. They are flawed, but they are still the main influence in the life of their child or teen. While the relationship changes from utter dependence as a baby to the broadening of influence from peers and additional adults through the teen years, the importance of a parent stays strong.

Scripture continually talks about children as members of their household unit. From the first family to the Israelite nation to the families encountering Jesus and the disciples writing to church communities, children are referenced in relation to their families. Households are saved and baptised and host churches in their home. I see children and teens as integral to their family unit.

If I believe that God's biblical plan is for children and teens to be embedded in a family, who are knitted into extended family and friends, who are in turn surrounded by a loving church community, then I do not have the luxury of dismissing parents if they aren't Christians.

We as a church are quick to set aside parents when it comes to their role in developing their child's faith. If a parent isn't a Christian, we often just bypass them and go straight for their child when it comes to spiritual input. I'm not convinced that this is God's best for children, teens or their parents.

As a representative of the church, my role is to see families flourishing in all areas, including their spiritual lives. When I hold myself accountable to honour the spiritual role of parents, whether or not they know they have it, my strategy and approach to them changes. While my heart longs for every child in this nation to love God sincerely and know his love in return, and live full of purpose and confidence, I also believe that God wants them to flourish spiritually in their family. It's my job to serve that vision as well.

So how do we still do outreach to children and teens, while also honouring and integrating their parents?

It's helpful to consider the two different spheres where we encounter non-Christian families:

At gathered events: our Christmas services, baptisms, funerals, weddings, outreach family events or tots groups – anytime we encounter families together.
2 Through relationship with the children or teens that we regularly input into on their own: school work, after-school clubs, youth events and groups.

## Gathered events

There are many times in the rhythms of our church ministry when we have access to fringe families as a whole: Christmas and Easter services, baptisms, funerals, weddings, outreach family events or tots groups. With a few adjustments, we can utilise these times to envision and equip these parents, as well as influence their children.

### Side-by-side experiences

In Chapter 7 we discussed how to use side-by-side experiences to equip parents and carers with core parenting-for-faith skills. When dealing with a significant amount of non-Christian parents in the mix, we need a slightly different focus, because often these parents are not looking to grow those skills. The opportunity we have is to give them a glimpse of what God has for them and their family and invite them to experience it. Often we are so focused on events being enjoyable, significant and imparting a specific knowledge that we miss the opportunity to allow families to explore something of God side by side, and in doing so, discover something new for their family.

These side-by-side experiences need to have three things:

1 a clear glimpse into something of God that we want them to understand and experience
2 an invitation to individually try something with God, side by side, to engage with that understanding
3 guidance on how to continue that

For example, we have done multiple services at Christmas including families with non-Christian parents, that focused on God's being 'with us'.

1 *Clear glimpse* – We gave families a glimpse into what 'God with us' means to others. At one service, we invited a few church individuals up to tell stories of when in the past year they relied on knowing that God was with them, through illness, job loss, the joy of a new birth and in ordinary life. This included two families who shared what 'God with them' looked like when the children were being bullied at school and through a season of night terrors. At another service, we invited people to bring in artwork showing what 'God with us' meant to them. We had contributions from all ages, and families were able to join in as the entire congregation looked around the room, before and after. The artwork gave a vision to those who had never thought about what God looks like in the midst of a school run or living with cancer. It enabled them to have a glimpse into life with God as a family. The glimpse began to build the vision and gave them something tangible and easy to talk about when they went home.

2 *Invitation* – Instead of just leading an intercession at the end of the sermon, we allowed space for a moment of engagement with God. We simply ended the sermon with a short prayer of thanks that God is with us always, and invited each person to tell God, either in their mind, by whispering to him or in writing, where in their life they need to know that God is with them. We gave them all a few silent seconds to connect. We then gave out well-made baubles that said: 'God is here'. I hoped this simple bauble would act as a springboard resource.

3 *How to continue* – Before the final songs, we encouraged everyone with the fact that at any moment they were feeling afraid, alone or lost they could connect with the God who was already with them by doing exactly what they had just done. This simple suggestion enabled parents to take away a skill that they had already tried, and that their child already knew, and be confident to use it. When I work with established Christian families, I try to give parents next

steps – ways to build on their experience. But with a significant amount of non-Christian families present, I merely encouraged them to repeat and adapt rather than try to cast a 'do it bigger' vision.

This simple equipping significantly impacted those who attended. In the following months, as I bumped into people from our estate on the road, they would tell me stories. One dad said that whenever his children were afraid, he would do 'that thing we did at Christmas' with them. 'You know, I actually think God helps or something,' he told me. I said he was awesome to help his kids connect with God like that and asked him how he felt when he did it. He said, 'I feel like I'm actually helping them with the spiritual bit of them too. I feel like a good dad.'

Other parents on the estate began to harass me for baubles every year as it made them feel 'warm and happy' when they saw the words 'God is here'. One parent told me that she didn't know much about God that she could tell her kids, but she did assure them that 'God is here'. 'It's like telling the truth. Makes us all think about God being in our house.' Another family said that it was fun, 'as whenever we watch TV at Christmas, our kids are like, "hey wanna watch TV with us, God, cause you know, he's here." And we are like, "yeah cool."'

Another time, we ran a men's all-age event, where local dads, grandads, older brothers and family friends could bring any male teen or child in their life. Hordes of men appeared, a good mix of churched and unchurched families. At one point in the event, I created a space for the men to pray with each other. I introduced it by saying that we believe that God is powerful and loves us and we wanted to create space for people to pray for each other. If people were comfortable to pray for the other person, they should feel free; if they weren't comfortable, then I encouraged them to bless the other person. I explained that 'bless' just means to put their hand on that person, look them in the eyes and say out loud what they hope God would do for that person. If they weren't comfortable with that, then feel free to just go for a hug. It was their choice. I told them all that we believed that a father's blessing is a powerful thing, and I encouraged those who were fathers or in a fathering role to bless the children and teens in their lives as much as they could. Some of the boys and teens had been in our clubs and prayed for the men in their lives, while the older men blessed them back. Several teary-eyed participants came up to me afterwards to tell me that that experience was among the most emotional in their lives. Years later, I ran into a man who said that after that experience he blessed his son every night, and ended up going on an Alpha course because he was so moved by the experience.

Some of these families began to show an interest in coming to a Parenting for Faith course, because they felt the purpose of God in their lives and saw how it impacted their kids. Sometimes seeing the impact of their small efforts to parent for faith makes them want to do it more. I try to encourage non-Christian families that to the extent that they have faith, wherever they are on their journey, they should share it with their children. Every little helps, and as the church we are here to cheer them on, equip them and enable them to meet the God who loves them and their kids.

If we can give non-Christian parents a glimpse of life with God when we gather together, let them try an experience with him, and enable them to keep that skill and feel empowered to use it, we not only share God but provide them with a new aspect of what it means to be a parent.

## Multigenerational community

One of the most powerful tools we have in envisioning and equipping fringe families is our multigenerational community. We can be so focused on running fantastic events that we forget the power of God's design: a child, surrounded by parents, knitted together with extended family and friends, surrounded by a loving, empowering multigenerational church community. If we want non-Christian families to catch a glimpse of God's design for their lives, then it is crucial for them to encounter the love and joy of our community.

Often we nominally do that by creating space for people to casually interact with each other. While many of us have people in our churches who are powerhouses of welcome, it can help for us to facilitate that connection in more deliberate ways. For example, if you are a church who baptises children, create a 'Get to know you' board for the families, so that as people come into the church they can read about the families and recognise them. Have a book out for each of the children so that congregation members can write verses, prayers, kind words and encouragements. I've known churches to have a canvas to which each member of the church adds their fingerprint, as an expression of God's love for the child and their belonging to the church. For other gatherings, I've known churches to ask every member family of the church to adopt a new family during big events, so that no new family is ever alone or unsure of what to do. Often this means that if the new family returns, they are recognised and a relationship develops.

We can create a culture where our church community makes such a statement of welcome and love that families truly feel at home.

## When our primary connection is with a child or teen

In some ways, using gathered events to connect with non-Christian parents is easy. We can equip them directly, and help them feel like they belong and are loved within community. But what about when we have little to no contact with parents, such as when we are running clubs or going into schools?

## Communication is key

I will forever remember the betrayed face of a parent who came to challenge me after one of the first after-school clubs I ever ran. 'What are you teaching my children?' the parent demanded 'They are coming home talking about God, and prayer, and sin, and have all these questions. I thought this was just an after-school club run by a church, not a brainwash-kids club!'

For many of us who work with unchurched children in the community, finding the right balance of spiritual input and just plain fun can be tricky. If the club contains any element of discipleship, we can find ourselves in a tenuous position, especially in youth groups. We are directly teaching spiritual things to children or teens, and facilitating them developing a connection with God, most of the time with no reference to the parents. How do we do this well?

Parents value their influence in their children's lives. It is scary for them to consider that people they don't know are taking their children and teaching them things that they might not know about or agree with. They don't want their children manipulated or taken advantage of. For the parents of teenagers, they feel like they have even less control of their children and religion can be a confusing and unexpected twist for them.

One of the most significant things we can do to honour parents' spiritual place in their children's lives is to be as open as possible about what is happening in our groups. When you create flyers or advertisements, be blatant about the spiritual content of the group. If you can, create a curriculum summary that is available by the drop-off door or, even better, on a website. Consistently invite parents to stay and participate. The more parents feel that we are open and available, with nothing to hide, the more they can feel comfortable that we aren't trying to steal their children's affections and common sense.

## Invest in relationships with parents

In many situations, such as schools work, we don't ever meet the parents of the children we engage with and we can feel isolated. One team that I worked with decided to solve this problem by attempting a lot of different avenues of relationship. They started hanging out at the school gates during drop-off once a week so that their faces would become familiar. They volunteered in classrooms and went on school trips. They volunteered for parent events like school fundraising and offered to host events at the church for free. They did lots of babysitting for families and got themselves invited to people's houses for food. They also hand-delivered encouragement packs to students going into their first year of secondary school. They invested so heavily into the relationships with the parents, alongside many others from our church, that over one-third of our Sunday-morning families came from our local school, primarily through feeling honoured and loved by the effort of these women and others at our church.

When it comes to clubs, I know churches who always have one person rostered to hang out outside the entire time, chatting to parents and families. One church I know of actually ran a parents' cafe at the club and had a team dedicated to building relationships there.

A few years ago, we began to meet many young people on street corners and invited them into our youth clubs. We opted to walk some of them home after the group and met their parents there. We became so consistent at getting them home safely, that when one of the youth became a Christian, and his behaviour began to change, his mum felt free to swing by the office to hear more about Jesus and Christianity because she was so shocked at the change in him. Their whole family began attending their local church, and she began to ask how to talk to her kid about God when she felt she knew less than he did. We were able to help them grow together, and help her feel confident in her journey. But had we not built that relationship with her, I think her reaction would have been more suspicion than excitement.

So, invest in those parent relationships and find creative ways of getting to know them, remembering what is happening in their lives and pastorally caring for them as well as their children.

## Have a natural next step in mind

For a while, I tried to create formal events or streamlined progressions for parents to go on. I'd run a youth club and then hold a barbecue at the end, as that would logically be the next step to invite parents to. Then, at the barbecue, I would invite them to an Easter fun day. I would try to manage parents through my programme to enable me to gain influence.

What I grew to understand is that I needed to take the Ikea approach. As I got to know these non-Christian parents, I would begin to get a sense of what would be a natural next step for them and would know what to mention. One family was immediately intrigued by the church weekend away, where one dad really enjoyed talking to one of our team, and the next step for them was to head to the pub. For others, it was sheer success to get a full conversation. One group of mums ended up demanding a Parenting for Faith course designed just around their questions. There is no one right way to envision and train non-Christian parents. As we get to know them, let's be open to what is the next step for them and help them to take it. But when we commit in our hearts to honouring them and not giving up on them being impactful in their children's life now and in the future, then we can see whole families go on the journey of faith together.

# Frequently asked questions

**When should we start equipping people to parent for faith? Should we be running a baby night?**

Personally, I would like to see the skills of parenting for faith being taught as a regular part of discipleship in a church. In essence, these skills are very similar to those of sharing your faith with people in everyday life. I hope that as our church cultures shift, we will be raising teenagers and young adults who already have the skills they need to parent well. Those who are soon to become parents often begin to think about how to parent for faith, so that is a perfect time to start investing in them. Check out **parentingforfaith.org** for helpful resources.

**We have a lot of parents of young adults. Is there any way I should be supporting them?**

It is never too late to start parenting for faith. Parents never stop parenting, and the more we acknowledge and support parents of all ages, the more transformations we will see. You may need to be proactive to individually connect with these parents, but when you do you will find that they genuinely love their children and are still trying to figure out how to parent their children for faith. Come alongside them, invite them into community, enable them to share their experience with others, and keep investing in them and encouraging them to not give up in trying to parent for faith.

**I seem to be getting only parents coming to our events. How do I encourage the extended family and congregation members to get involved too?**

This is a common problem, and the solution lies with how we describe parenting for faith. I almost always use the phrase 'all those who influence children' and even list the types of people who are welcome to attend: aunts, godparents, grandparents, children's and youth leaders, etc. I find a good sermon about God's design for children's discipleship and their place within it can often give permission for those extended families to begin to invest. Also, have a look at the parenting-for-faith stories being told through services or social media: if they are primarily parent stories, then you may need to better envision the community.

**What about grandparents? How do we support them to be spiritually significant in the lives of their grandchildren?**

Grandparents are a vital part of the spiritual development of children and teens, so it is important that we invest in equipping them as well. Some of the grandparents we encounter are excited about their second round of parenting for faith, while others are hurting about the choices their children have made and are in the awkward position of wanting to help their grandchildren connect with God when their children might not be open to that. The skills of parenting for faith, of connection, positioning, discipleship and prayer, are the same skills that grandparents and others use. They tend not to need different skills, but they may benefit from one-off nights to enable them to talk through the particular complexities of grandparenting for faith while also respecting their children's wishes. As long as you make it clear that grandparents are vital to their grandchildren's spiritual development and that all parenting-for-faith events include them, you will find that they will come and be a welcome addition to the community exploring this together.

**We have a large proportion of children with additional needs in our church. How do I equip those parents to help their children connect with God?**

First, it is important that we are speaking the truth to parents and our church communities that children and teens with additional needs can and do have lifelong connections with God, no matter what the severity of their needs are. As with all families, our role is to help give parents the skills they need to help their unique children connect with God in the everyday, in whatever way it looks for them. To help you with this, search 'additional needs' on **parentingforfaith.org** and you will find videos and connections to people who specialise in supporting and equipping parents of children with additional needs, including how to help them parent for faith well.

**How do I support a family where one partner is a Christian and the other isn't?**

Often some of the conflict between parents occurs when it comes to 'controlling' their children into religious behaviour, or when they want to do corporate acts of worship at home. The skills that we give parents is about them allowing their children to see what their relationship with God looks like, to explain spiritual things in a normal way and to create an open space for their children to connect with God for themselves. Because of this, we find that the conflict about controlling children may be less when parents begin to shift to these different skills. In order to support these families well, I find it is really helpful to treat the non-Christian partner with as much honour as I can, including them in social situations, investing in the relationship as much as they are comfortable with and reminding myself that they too are spiritually significant in the life of their child. I make sure that I am treating them as proactively as I do other non-churched parents, as it is easy to default into ignoring them as they drift around the edges.

**The parents at my church keep asking me whether they should make their teenagers come to church. What do I tell them?**

It is the classic question that we all must face. For each child the answer will vary. The problem is often connected to the misunderstanding that 'church' means the church service. When parents are empowered to talk to their children about the church as a whole, they often find a suitable solution between them. Check out Session 8 of the Parenting for Faith course for how to help children and young people connect with church.

**I'm a leader in the church, but I don't feel that I'm very good at parenting my kids for faith. How could I equip others?**

We are all on a journey of learning how to parent our children for faith. Helping others on their journey as you are on yours is absolutely fine. You aren't saying, 'Parent like me'; you are saying, 'I am on my journey and you are on yours, let's learn together.' We have resources specially designed for church leaders, as we know that parenting as a church leader requires an additional set of skills. Visit **parentingforfaith.org** for the resources and events we have for you.

**How do I help engage families in worship?**

This is a huge question and one that cannot be answered fully, as it ultimately depends on the current circumstances at your church. Each church is different, so the reasons behind families struggling in worship will be different. I often approach a topic by thinking about hindrances. This word 'hindered' is significant for us who serve parents. Scripture uses many different words for 'hinder'. Two of the most significant for us are:

1   being proactively held back (e.g. Luke 11:52)
2   having something in your way that can trip, entangle or be an obstacle (e.g. Hebrews 12:1).[7]

My first step would be to ask what is either holding parents back or getting in their way of worshipping together at church. Are the parents struggling with discipline? Are their children coming not expecting to engage? Is the leader not helping to facilitate, or do the parents not know how to equip their children to worship and encourage them as they do? Are the parents themselves not worshippers, so don't know what to do personally, much less know how to help their children? Once I know what the hindrances are, I can go about removing them.

We've looked at many methods in this book for envisioning parents that it is possible, giving them the skills they need to coach their children, as well as how to create space for those skills to grow in the main service. In particular look at Sessions 6 and 8 of the Parenting for Faith course on **parentingforfaith.org**, which discuss, respectively, how to proactively disciple our children as well as how to help them engage with church.

### How do I create a springboard resource?

When you create or adapt a springboard resource, it is important that it does not end up doing the work for the parents. The purpose of a springboard is to facilitate parents to use their skills, not to replace those skills. To achieve this, think through four questions.

1   *What is the barrier that is hindering parents, carers or extended families?* This question is crucial, as it focuses us on the purpose behind the springboard resource. Sometimes we pour endless time into creating something for parents to use when there isn't a burning need for it. Unless parents need additional help because they are being hindered, I tend not to give them a resource.

2   *What skills am I setting up parents to learn or use?* Springboard resources are to enable parents, carers and extended families to use or learn some of the core parenting-for-faith skills. Ensuring that the resource maximises parents using their skills prevents us from accidentally creating something that takes over from the parent. Knowing what skills we want them to use shapes the opportunities we create.

3   *What is my launch point?* A key factor of springboard resources is restraint. Springboard resources stop short of dictating everything that happens. It gets parents only as far as just past the barrier and then stops, enabling the parent, carer or extended family member to take it to the next stage. So, when we create these resources, we always need to be asking ourselves, 'At what point do I need to get out of the way?'

4   *What fruit is intended to come out of this?* When families use the resources, we want them to be able to walk away genuinely blessed by the spiritual fruit that comes from it. The resources cannot be merely a technique to get a parent to do something. Springboard resources need to facilitate a spiritual moment that makes parents and children feel that something small but significant happened, and they both were part of it.

These questions can apply to anything that you create. One of my recent books utilises this approach. *Comfort in the Darkness* is a book of stories focused on the night, sleep and dreams designed for parents to read to their children. It came about as a springboard resource.[8] For that book, the questions looked like this:

1   *What is the barrier that is hindering parents, carers or extended families?* Children are scared of the dark and parents often do not know how to bring peace to their children. Their techniques aren't working, and they feel powerless.

2   *What skills am I setting up parents to learn or use?* How to verbally frame and explain what is spiritually happening; creating windows into their lives with God; conversational prayer; curious questions. (All core skills I teach through the course and other books.)

3 *What is my launch point?* The book will provide the biblical basis
  for a new way of thinking about the night, but its application
  section will be deliberately open-ended. There will be questions
  that have no right answers, leaving parents to have to navigate
  tough questions with their child, and questions that provide
  opportunities for parents to explain their journeys with God.
  There also will be suggestions for conversational prayer moments
  that leave parents to decide how to proceed and process the
  connection moments.
4 *What fruit is intended to come out of this?* Children will be more
  peaceful at night, and parents will feel more confident to respond
  to their children's fears because they will have gained a mutual
  biblical foundation, and feel comfortable using new skills in the
  night-time context.

These questions can apply to anything that you create. Not all
barriers that parents experience will require a springboard resource.
As we discussed in Chapter 6, some parents may need you to teach
them a new skill or facilitate a conversation. But there will be times
when a springboard resource is required. It doesn't have to be pretty
or well-presented. The goal is to get parents over a wall, not to create
a wonderful, beautiful performance piece of a resource. Be bold!

**How do I teach in a way that enables parents and children to learn
side by side? How do I create an all-age talk?**

While there is no formula for crafting a great all-age talk to enable
parents, teens and children to learn alongside each other, there are
some guiding principles to shaping something impactful.

1 *Don't aim for a specific age group.* As soon as you begin to think of
  aiming it at seven-year-olds so that it's accessible to people of all
  ages, you have lost the impact of what you are supposed to do. A
  great talk is accessible to all ages because it is well done and holds
  to the other principles. Forget about age groups.

2  *One jump.* Many people write sermons like they are taking their
   congregations on stepping stones across a river: Point A sets up
   Point B which lays the transition to Point C, which nicely leads on
   to Point D and so on. For me, that wastes time and effort when
   you are teaching adults and children together. One jump is all
   I allow myself. Point A leads to Point B. That's it. No three-point
   sermons. No explaining something that reveals something else
   that ultimately means this truth, which applies in this way.
   One jump. Jesus did this all the time with the parables. 'Hear
   the story of the pearl of great price? God's kingdom is like
   that.' He would say something and mean that one thing.
   His simplicity of teaching made him a draw for all ages.
   The key question then becomes: what is the one point I want
   everyone to walk away with? What is the one truth that this is
   about, and how do I set it up so it only takes one jump to get there?

3  *Get everyone off-footed.* Most all-age talks tend to cover familiar
   ground. Naturally, that drives anyone who has heard the story
   or explored the topic to boredom before you've even begun.
   If you say 'David and Goliath', most of the older generation
   will instantly tune out and so will a lot of the children. This
   means that the adults and children are no longer learning
   alongside each other. If the goal is side-by-side learning and
   experience, then I need to make sure both adults and children
   are experiencing this from the same starting point. To do
   this, I need to create talks that genuinely intrigue all ages.
   The simple way to do this is to choose topics and stories from
   the Bible that aren't usually covered: for example, the story
   of Jehoshaphat – a beautiful one about trust and all ages
   standing in faith together – or the story of a girl called Noah
   (Zelophehad's daughter – Numbers 27), who with her sisters
   challenged the tradition of her people, which led to God changing
   the law. There are many excellent stories in the Bible that we
   almost never use, so when we do it makes the whole room
   tune in because everyone is ready to learn something new.
   If I have to talk about a more frequently covered topic, I try to take
   an unusual angle. For example, if I was doing the armour of God,

I might look at the combat styles of the time and run experiments about the functionality of the armour in a battle scenario. When we present something simply (with one jump), and yet it feels new to most people, we create a natural engagement that in other cases we would have to work hard to gain.

4 *Make them laugh.* I have no science on this, but in my experience people learn better when they are laughing, so I try to include joy as part of all-age talks. This does not mean games, which rarely result in the kind of joy that I'm talking about. Have you ever watched a comedy special on television and seen the shots of the audience? Their faces are full of sheer joy, and they sometimes look at each other as they are reminded of something; it is pure happiness. If we can achieve moments of real enjoyment, I find it to be very helpful. I have my techniques for achieving that, and you will have yours, but try to put away games and create real enjoyment and delight.

5 *Always have them try the application in the room.* If I'm going to present to adults and children something new about God, some new way of walking with him, then I need to give them the opportunity to experience that while they are in the room. This enables parents to learn how to lead into it, helps all the congregation respond to God, and gives the children and young people confidence in adding that experience to their growing number of ways to walk with God.

## How do I tell other people's stories?

As we gain experience in working with parents, we begin to collect stories, sometimes accidentally. We hear the stories that people share after church or during a course, and they stay in our memory. As we continue to support parents and lead events, we may want to share these stories to equip or encourage other parents. So, how do we tell these stories in a way that honours the people who shared them with us, while also being useful for those we are sharing it with?

- *Don't use names.* When we share stories, it is to use as an example or to offer encouragement. It isn't to put anybody up on a pedestal or expose them in any way. Because of that I never use names.

- *Ask permission.* If you ever want to tell a story to people, whether personally or publicly, get permission from the person or family whose story it is. If you are going to tell the story publicly, also get permission from the children. I am happy either for the parents to ask the child for me or, if they prefer, for me to do it. This is important, because even though I would avoid using their names, the children themselves may recognise the story and feel exposed. And seek this permission with an open heart to it being refused. There are many stories that I am desperate to use, but either the parents or often the children do not want me to, and I respect that. This is a very sensitive part of people's lives, and they must feel in control of their stories and feel safe in your confidentiality.

- *Tell the fruit as much as you can.* Often we can tell stories as examples of how to parent for faith, so the focus quickly shifts to the doing or performing of parenting for faith. This can lead parents to think that there is a standard of parenting for faith that they should be held to. When you tell a story, don't just say, 'I know a parent who did this' or 'Here is a story of someone who did it brilliantly.' Keep the fruit at the forefront: 'There was one kid who was struggling with bullying, and his parents tried lots of things to try to help him process it spiritually. What ended up bringing the kid a lot of peace and making him surprisingly confident in God was… The kid spiritually ended up in a wonderful place because of it.'

- *Keep a record.* Once you get going, you will run across stories to use everywhere. It's overwhelming at the end of the week to think, 'Oh, someone said a good thing about sports and choosing… Oh, I can't remember who… Argh!' I keep a file on my computer, so that as I listen to parents I can jot down the stories and then follow up. Sometimes I follow up so that I can facilitate them sharing the story themselves; other times, so that they can record it to share or so I can ask for permission to tell the story at the next course to encourage other parents.

**I feel like no matter how much I try, the parents and carers I work with seem really disengaged. What do I do?**

First, investigate why they are disengaged. Have some conversations to tease out their thinking. Is it because they firmly believe that the church should be the primary spiritual disciplers? If so, it looks like the church leadership need to integrate some teaching into the preaching programme. If they are just tired, the first step could be to get them some support. If they have a low value for the spiritual aspect of their children's lives, then start giving them a vision of what is possible, using those skills of Ikea, truth-telling and the community stories. Sometimes disengaged parents just need to be allowed to join the flow of others, so focus on going with those parents, grandparents or extended family who are interested. The first Parenting for Faith course I ran I had three people. They didn't all show up each week, so some weeks it was just a mother of two boys in their 20s and me chatting in a big room. But those three were enthusiastic, and the next course was bigger. Then our children's ministry leaders got on board, and it grew from there. Go with those that are going, and cast the vision wide.

# **Acknowledgements**

My son, Caleb – thank you for being such a wonderful encourager as I wrote this book. You helped me not to get distracted, pushed courage into my heart with your words, prayed for me and even sacrificed some of our playtime so I could finish this book. Thank you for being team with me. I love you.

My mother, Susan – thank you for teaching me how to be a better writer and for walking with me on these agonising birthing journeys of bringing books into the world. I am ever grateful for your time, love, skill and wisdom.

My father, Terry – thank you for making me laugh and always encouraging me to dig deeper with perseverance. It is an honour to be your daughter.

My husband, Mark – thank you for listening to me talk for hours while I found the words to write. Your patience with me is superhuman.

Annie Willmot – thank you for being next to me, helping to shape this book. It is such a blessing to be doing ministry with you.

Becky Sedgwick, Richard Fisher, Bill Lattimer and the BRF team – thank you for believing in Parenting for Faith and bringing your skills, gifts, time and effort to strengthen it and partner with it. I am humbled to be working with you.

For my friends who have answered texts, encouraged me to keep going and put up with me when I'm in 'Book World', thank you for your friendship – Jo and Elliot Ireton, Andrea Johnson, Susie and James Yeates, John and Kate Payne, Elaine Webster, and Adam and Jess Price.

And finally, to Daisy and Charlie at Nando's – thank you for letting me type at Table 19 for hours and hours and welcoming me every time.

# Notes

1    Olwyn Mark, *Passing on Faith* (Theos, 2016).
2    'Faith in our families', research report (Care for the Family and Hope, 2017), careforthefamily.org.uk/wp-content/uploads/2017/03/Faith-in-our-Families-Research-booklet.pdf
3    Rachel Turner, *Parenting Children for a Life of Faith: Helping children meet and know God*, omnibus edition (BRF, 2018). This is a revised and updated edition of three previously published titles: *Parenting Children for a Life of Faith*, *Parenting Children for a Life of Purpose* and *Parenting Children for a Life of Confidence*.
4    Lynn Alexander, *Children, Families and God: Drawing the generations together to change the world* (Lynn Alexander, 2012).
5    Freely available from parentingforfaith.org
6    For more on what skills to give parents to help their children discover their personal purpose and their place in the wider body of Christ, as well as how we integrate children and young people into our church teams, see Turner, *Parenting Children for a Life of Purpose*.
7    The Greek word used in Luke 11:52 is the same word that the gospel writers use when Jesus told the disciples not to hinder the children who were coming to him (Luke 18:16); it speaks of proactive restraining or stopping. The Greek word translated 'hinder' in Hebrews 12:1 refers to impediments that get in the way, and may have referred to things that people were wearing.
8    Rachel Turner, *Comfort in the Darkness: Helping children draw close to God through biblical stories of night-time and sleep* (BRF, 2016).

# parenting for faith

## Inspiring and equipping parents

BRF's Parenting for Faith programme provides resources and training for parents, communities and churches to support them in bringing up children in the Christian faith.

Find out more at **parentingforfaith.org.uk**

 brf.org.uk